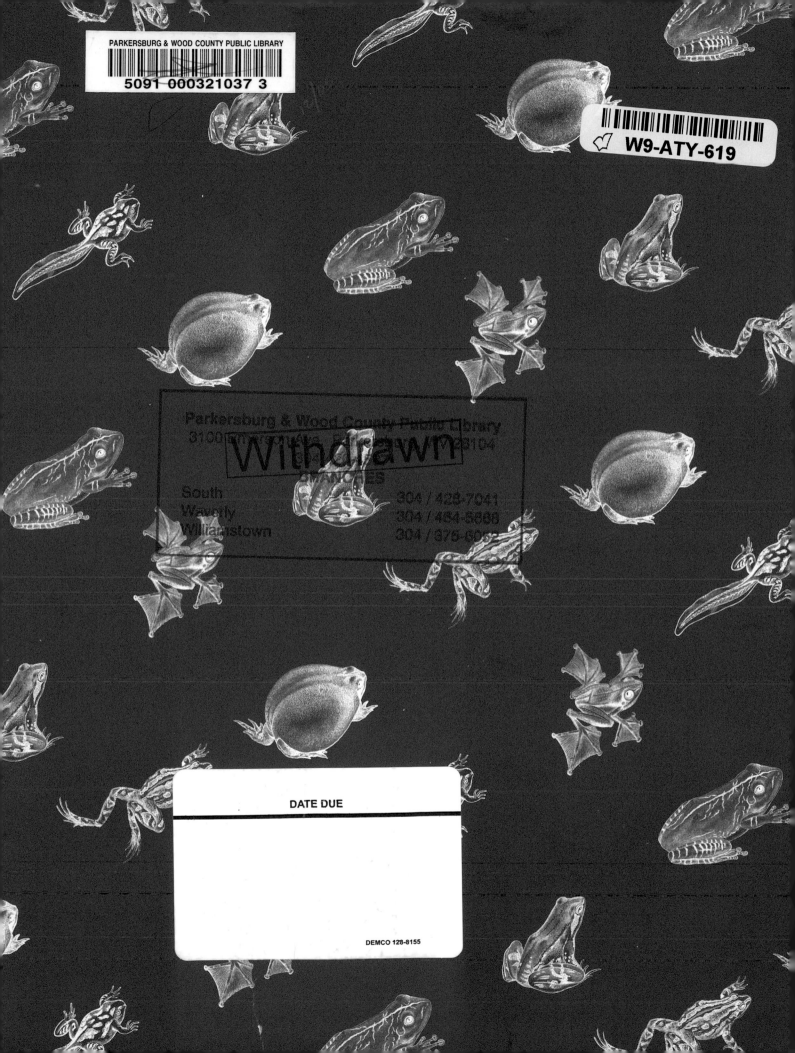

FROGS

FROGS
INSIDE THEIR REMARKABLE WORLD

Ellin Beltz

FIREFLY BOOKS

Contents

Acknowledgments

FROGS HAVE ALWAYS BEEN VERY SPECIAL TO ME. I recall getting in great trouble at summer camp because I left the group and was found soaking wet in the swamp, staring deep into the eyes of a calling frog.

Fortunately for me, first my parents, then my husband and daughter, tolerated or enjoyed all the hopping, slithering, wriggling and scritching that accompanied the wide variety of animals captured for photographs and scientific specimens or given to me by a variety of keepers, breeders and veterinarians.

Keeping amphibians where you can see them all the time helps you imagine what they are doing in the wild. To study frogs, you learn how to stay up late and sleep in the daytime. Your friends are likewise nocturnal and your neighbors think you work the swing shift. I'd like to thank some of the many people with whom I have spent dark and stormy nights, including Daria-Jean Sullivan, Marla Johnson, Frank "Nicky" Nolan, Ken Mierzwa, Eloise Beltz-Decker, Stan Tyson, Steve Barten, Steve Busack, Julian Bentley, Marco Mendez, Teri Radke, Jon Meyers, Sheri Janowski, Doug Mansker and Barbara Shelonzek.

Learning about amphibians in college and graduate school included delightful classroom and field experiences led by Drs. Eugene McArdle, Robert Betz, Albert Forslev, Hansa Upadhyay, Christopher T. Ledvina, Charles Shabica and Ms. Rita Keefe.

Learning your passion is insufficient; you must take every opportunity to record and transmit it. I would like to thank Michael A. Dloogatch, Sean McKeown, Joseph and Suzanne Collins, Charles Bogert, Hobart Smith, Roger Conant, Karen Furnweger, Valerie DuPrez, Mike Pingleton, Ray Novotny, Holly Collins, David Conrad, Laura Sanders, Gary VanDyke, Gabrielle Lyon, Paul Sereno, Northeastern Illinois University, Trinity Christian College, College of the Redwoods, the Field Museum of Natural History, University of Chicago, Project Exploration, and the Morton Arboretum for outreach opportunities. Without them, I would have never had the communication skills and confidence to give programs and write and publish my work.

←← Poison frogs, like these inch-long (2.5 cm) Strawberry poison frogs, *Dendrobates pumilo*, are so named because they produce some of the most potent toxins known to science.

Special thanks are also due Ann B. Abid, Kraig Adler, David Cannatella, Joseph T. Collins, Darrel Frost, James Harding, Ami Hendrici, Raymond Hoser, Judi McCoy, John Lowerison, Marco Mendez, Robert Murphy, Caroline Seawright, Rick Speare, Michael J. Tyler, Romulus Whitaker, Janaki Lenin, Spanky McFarland, Larry Rust, Lux Interior and Poison Ivy for invaluable last-minute assistance, inspiration, encouragement and information during the research and writing process.

In addition to book, magazine, journal and Internet sources, I have eighteen years' worth of more obscure frog resources provided by regular contributors to my column in *The Bulletin of the Chicago Herpetological Society*, including Bill Burnett, Mike Dloogatch, C. Kenneth Dodd, Alan Rigerman, Wes von Papineäu, Allen Salzberg, Ms. G.E. Chow, Mark Witwer, Ray Boldt, Claus Sutor, James Harding, Lori King, Tom Taylor, James N. Stuart, David Blatchford, Marty Marcus, Patricia and Paul L. Beltz and self-described "frog-lover" MaryBeth Trilling.

Authors alone do not make books; their lives are inextricably intertwined in the creative process. Throughout this effort, I have been supported by family, friends and coworkers, including Ken Mierzwa, Hobart Brown, Lisa Samuels, Deborah Addington, Lawrence Alvarado, Ed Greenwood, Elisabeth Crane, Eva Lyons, Beorn Zapp, Charlie Jordan, Burrill Catanach, Bob Doran, Emily Gurnon, Sharon Bonino, Ken Torbert, Mike Rafter, Bill Abens and Marilyn McCormick. On the professional side, my personal thanks to members of the production team directed by Michael Worek and Brad Wilson at Firefly Books including my patient and interested editor Dan Liebman and innovative designer Gareth Lind, as well as proofreader Deborah Viets.

I would like to thank the Pacific treefrogs, *Pseudacris regilla*, who sang "ribbet, ribbet" from the damp rhododendrons around our Victorian cottage in a seaside village in far northwestern California while I was writing the last half of this book. Their unceasing encouragement reminded me to keep writing, especially on rainy, dark days and late in the night.

Years too late for him to see the effects of his encouragement, I'd like to dedicate this work to the late Angus Bellairs, for his inspiration at and after the First World Congress of Herpetology in 1989 at Canterbury, England. Angus proved that one of the most prominent herpetologists in the English-speaking world could share his knowledge in a way that interested everyone – from young schoolboys like Julian Bentley to prominent members of his highly specialized profession like Drs. Bill Duellman and Linda Trueb – without losing their attention. For not only was Angus informative, he was highly entertaining. No one who ever heard his stories of frog hunting during live warfare in the middle of the 20th century will ever forget a word! May I interest you as much as he did me.

And last, but certainly not least, thank you for reading my book.

Ellin Beltz
Ferndale, California

Introduction

WHY ARE HUMANS FASCINATED BY FROGS? What is a frog but a little bundle of matter and energy? Is it perhaps that frogs look and act rather like people? They sing and cavort, court, mate and raise families all in plain view of the humans with whom they share their world.

Frogs let it all hang out. From their enthusiastic breeding assemblages to their long tongues, they let us see their every move – even if we don't understand what we see.

Frogs teach us that the more we learn, the more we find out we need to know. Much of what we're learning about frogs directly relates to human physiology and habitat requirements. Perhaps the most important thing is that while there are limits within which individual organisms can function, as a group frogs exist to break their own rules.

One study logged over a thousand food items disappearing into a toad in one day, but others show that some frogs can go six months or more without eating in the hottest deserts. While most frogs prefer just about the same temperatures as people, others can freeze nearly solid and revive without damage in cold northerly climes. Some frogs nervously vanish at the slightest sound while others sit patiently for examination. And, as everyone knows, some frog species are disappearing while others extend their ranges worldwide.

Although each chapter has its own introduction, here are some frequently asked questions – with answers – that introduce the concepts of the book in a general manner.

← Classically frog shaped, this northern leopard frog, *Rana pipiens*, has both eyes on guard for predators. After breeding season, they roam far from water in damp meadows, where morning dew rehydrates them.

Why study frogs by family?

Including live and fossil frogs, there are somewhere between 4,000 and 5,000 species known, with more discovered every year as formerly remote jungles and rock outcrops are explored and studied. At a minimum, using family organization reduces the need for range maps and repetitive text.

Long ago, people discovered that it is easier to learn things by first seeing generalities and then becoming more and more specific. We study nature by dividing it into large groups by similarities and subdividing by differences. We recognize a large group of amphibians, divided into three groups: salamanders, caecilians and frogs. Within frogs are some 31 families, each one with its own set of characteristics, sometimes including habitat requirements, breeding patterns, behaviors and parenting methods.

How is this book different from a field guide?

Field guides provide a species-by-species account of every organism within their scope. At 4,000 to 5,000 species worldwide, a list of just the names of frog species, one to a line, could take a hundred pages of text!

Why include all the Latin names?

This book includes a list and discussion of frogs and toads by family. Some individual members of each family are discussed in detail and serve as representatives for their family in the text.

All the "difficult" Latin and Greek family names and species names have been included for several reasons:

1. Scientific names are used every day by people around the world in books and on the Internet.

2. "Common names" are not standardized. As people self-publish on the Internet, new common names are created and spread. The common names also use common words. A search of "parsley frogs" on the Internet found recipes for frog legs with parsley, but nothing on the frog family "Parsley Frogs" themselves.

3. Scientific names are the same in all nations and in all languages. They can be found in publications and on websites in foreign languages, even if you can't read the rest of the type.

How do you say the names?

To pronounce scientific names at least as well as anyone today, there are only three rules:

1. Look for familiar word parts that you know how to say. Words that begin with unusual consonants are from Greek. For example *Xenopus* ("alien foot") is easy for anyone who has ever used a famous brand of photocopier. Another Greek-influenced name was coined for *Pseudacris* treefrogs. Think "pseudonym" (false name) and say "*Pseud-acris.*"

2. For any unfamiliar word, imagine you are ordering Italian food or upscale coffee. Stretch out all the syllables and say each one. Try the eyeball-popping "*Disco-glossis*" ("round tongue"); or a real toughie, "*E-leuth-ero-dactyl-us*" ("free-fingers") for practice!

3. Be confident. No one has really spoken Latin for a very long time. You will hear several variants of each scientific name, particularly at international

conferences where it is interesting to hear how the scientific names pop out of languages that you otherwise do not understand at all.

What do the names mean?

Many word parts are used over and over again for amphibians and are also used for other groups. You can often find these word parts in an unabridged dictionary. Examples of these include "Batrach" for frogs, "gloss" for tongue, "limno" for marsh, and "dactyls" for fingers.

Some names were formed from sounds made by the frog. For example, "Ra-na" is the sound made by a southern European frog, so the Romans used *Rana* for all frogs. Also, the coqui frog's name reflects its loud "co-kee" cry.

Why don't you say "frogs and toads"?

All toads are frogs, so saying "frogs" covers all the families that contain animals commonly referred to as "toads." Researchers currently do not believe all the "toads" descend from a common ancestor; therefore, using a collective group name for an unrelated group creates confusion. Just search "difference between frogs and toads" on a search engine for 20 or more definitions. Each one is equally correct, but you have to consider the local "toad" known to the writer. There are, of course, differences between frogs and toads. You'll find these in a chart on page 41 in the chapter on Frog Families.

And finally...

What we can learn from frogs may be of great use to humans in our future. So far, frogs have been used in anatomical studies, as pregnancy tests before more modern chemical testing, and as models for developing radical treatments for burn patients. They have also served as inspiration for thousands of artists, writers and everyday people. And there is no doubt that they will continue to do so.

1 A Brief Natural History

CHAPTER ONE

A Brief Natural History

FROGS AND PEOPLE HAVE A LONG HISTORY. Ancient Egyptians used a character of a frog's profile to represent the number 100,000, and many other cultures painted, described and created stories around these plentiful little animals. The Romans called frogs *Rana* from the sound made by the local pond frogs, and their word for toad, *Bufo*, has entered English in the word "buffoon."

People used frogs as weather or seasonal indicators as well as for food and insect control for thousands of years before anyone even considered trying to find out how many different types of frogs and toads exist on Earth. To determine that number, a system of classification would be needed to prevent identical organisms from being counted twice.

Scientists classify plants and animals according to a system invented during the 1750s by a Swedish biologist, Carl von Linné, also known as Carl Linnaeus or Carolus Linnaeus, who is often called the Father of Taxonomy. Linné divided up plants and animals according to physical characteristics and used a hierarchical system that we now call binomial nomenclature. Each plant or animal is given a unique name.

Other people had tried to develop systems to organize all life on Earth. Linné's breakthrough idea was to start with large groups of similar things and then divide them into smaller and smaller groups until finally there was no further difference between individuals. He called this final, most specific group a "species."

Linné lived in exciting times, when new continents were being discovered by Europeans. Exploration teams often included naturalists who, in a burst of nationalistic fervor, collected specimens of all the new plants and animals and then sent them to their national museums. Several explorers also sent

← Edward Drinker Cope named them *Hyla callidryas* ("treefrog of the hot forest") in 1862. Later it was found that the red-eyed treefrogs really belong in the genus *Agalychnis*, but their species name, *callidryas*, remains unchanged. They are found from Mexico to Colombia in coastal lowlands.

←← Marine toad, *Bufo marinus*.

CLASSIFICATION OF THE BULLFROG, *RANA CATESBEIANA*

Kingdom Animalia – Animals
└ Phylum Chordata – Animals with a spinal cord
　└ Subphylum Vertebrata – Animals with a backbone
　　└ Class Amphibia – Amphibians
　　　└ Order Anura – Frogs and Toads
　　　　└ Family Ranidae – Ranid Frogs
　　　　　└ Genus *Rana*
　　　　　　└ Species *catesbeiana*

↑ American Bullfrog, *Rana catesbeiana*, swimming.

preserved specimens to Linné in Sweden. One of these men was an extra-ordinary traveler named Mark Catesby, who collected an American bullfrog in colonial America and sent it to Linné in Sweden. Linné named the bull-frog for Catesby and classified it *Rana catesbeiana* (as shown above).

After two and a half centuries of study, much of the life on Earth has been described. Many museums, government agencies, universities and individuals have participated in putting this knowledge in books and publications, and more recently, on the Internet.

The process of determining the relationships between organisms is called "taxonomy." Fossils and preserved dead amphibians were shipped to Europe and North America from around the world. Early taxonomists named new species according to appearance and anatomy only. The central idea of species, the ability to create fertile offspring, was ignored, and many invalid species' names entered the nomenclature.

New tools and technology are continually being developed and used to reconstruct the genealogical relationships of all life on Earth. Today, scientists around the world are studying not only the physical characters but also the genetic code that determines the internal and external characteristics described by classical taxonomists. A new philosophy of classification, called "phylogenetics," is used to determine genealogical relationships between species. Phylogenetics, which means "how the tree arose," is sometimes also called "cladistics," meaning the study of clades, or groups of organisms.

In this system, which has a clearly defined set of rules and terms, a group of organisms is a "taxon" (plural, "taxa"). Their common ancestor is at the root; the tree of life divides at a node and creates at least two branches. One or both of these branches divide again and again over time. Species occupy the terminal ends of branches. Groups of organisms that all had a single ancestor at one time in the past are called "monophyletic."

One of the big scientific issues now is whether the three groups of amphibians – the salamanders, the caecilians, and the frogs and toads – are all descended from one common ancestor called "Lissamphibia." If so, Amphibia is not only a natural group, but also a monophyletic taxon. (See the diagram on page 22.)

Life Before Amphibians

THE HISTORY OF LIFE on Earth is recorded in fossils found in rocks around the world. A diagram called "the geological time column" (see below) shows the relationship between all these times, even though nowhere on Earth is there one perfect place that records every minute of geological time. Instead, some parts of the world have older rocks, and some parts have younger rock formations.

The surface of the Earth is constantly changing. Some parts of the surface are ancient; other parts solidified just yesterday. New rock is made by volcanoes; old rock is recycled by weathering and tectonic forces. Because fossils require highly specific conditions for preservation, we have only a tiny sample of the huge diversity of life in the past.

Some of the best fossils we have are the results of catastrophic events such

GEOLOGICAL TIME COLUMN
(mya = millions of years ago)

Eon	Era	Period	Epoch	Begins (approx.)
Phanerozoic	Cenozoic	Quaternary	Recent	1 mya
			Pleistocene	2 mya
		Tertiary	Pliocene	5 mya
			Miocene	24 mya
			Oliogocene	37 mya
			Eocene	58 mya
			Paleocene	65 mya
	Mesozoic	Cretaceous		144 mya
		Jurassic		208 mya
		Triassic		250 mya
	Paleozoic	Permian		286 mya
		Carboniferous	Pennsylvanian	320 mya
			Mississippian	360 mya
		Devonian		408 mya
		Silurian		438 mya
		Ordovician		505 mya
		Cambrian		600 mya
Proterozoic	Precambrian			2,500 mya
Archaen				3,800 mya
Hadean				4,600 mya

as landslides, mudslides, volcanic ash deposits or sand blowouts. Some early geologists therefore believed that only catastrophic forces caused change on Earth. Others, however, insisted that only "slow but sure" processes led to the rise of life on Earth and its development over time. We now know that both these mechanisms – catastrophic forces and gradual processes – have contributed to the rise and fall of various forms of life, and to the preservation of their remains in the rock record over the vast span of geological time.

With the exception of the weird creatures found in the earliest Precambrian fossil faunas of Australian Ediacara and the Canadian Burgess Shale, most fossils can be placed in their appropriate taxon because they look similar to plants and animals we know today. The earliest life on Earth was marine, but eventual colonization of the land and air was certain and, by the Devonian, spiders roamed the land. Since modern spiders are predators, we can assume that other invertebrates inhabited the land as well.

At the same time, roughly 365 million years ago, the seas, bays, lakes and rivers were full of living things. One group of fish developed lungs and stiffened fins, making it the first four-legged vertebrate, called a "tetrapod." Curiously, tetrapods and fish move in exactly opposite ways. In fish, locomotion is provided by the body, with the tail propelling the fish through the water. In tetrapods, the legs are used for propulsion; the longer tetrapod tail is only for balance. The ability to breathe and move out of water may have let the earliest tetrapods move around the way that some modern fish do, allowing them to get to new water across land.

The lobe-finned fishes gave rise to the earliest fossil tetrapods, named

↓ **Primitive frogs had up to eight sets of ribs; modern frogs have few or none.**

FROGS

↑ The super-continent Pangaea was completed about 250 million years ago and began to break up about 180 million years before the present.

Ichthyostega and *Acanthostega*, whose fossils were found in East Greenland. Their skeletons show some major differences from those of their fish ancestors. They had light shoulders and pelvic girdles and had developed a neck, which let their heads move from side to side. Even so, they may have spent a lot of time in water.

During the Devonian, Greenland was in the tropics and land plants were forming the first forests. The continents were mostly joined in a giant land mass called "Pangaea," as seen in the map above. The northern part of Pangaea is called "Laurasia," and the southern part "Gondwana."

Tetrapods moved outward from their point of origin and colonized every suitable habitat they found. It took 135 million years or so, but they eventually reached the ends of their Earth – the piece of land we now call Antarctica. On the way, they diversified. New types of tetrapods developed to exploit specific habitats.

The largest of the new groups was called "Labyrinthodonts," after the mazelike patterns in their tooth enamel. Labyrinthodonts were large animals. One of the best known examples is called *Eryops*. It grew to about 6 feet (2 m) long and had a big bony head, strong limbs, a long tail and rows of sharp teeth in a large mouth. Many of its fossils have been dug up in Sydney, Australia, where they are described as short-limbed, long-bodied animals rather like crocodiles with fins on their tail. The Australians date their specimens to about 345 million years ago. Anatomical studies reveal that Labryrinthodonts probably could hear; there was a bone connecting the brain and a large opening covered by skin.

As usual with animal evolution, not all Labyrinthodonts were big. Many species evolved to fill most of the available habitat niches. Labyrinthodonts dominated the land for about 100 million years, during the Carboniferous and up to the end of the Permian.

Early Amphibian History

AT SOME POINT in their history, one subgroup of the Labyrinthodonts began to change; slowly and subtly their skeletons became lighter and more slender. This proposed ancestor of the modern frogs and toads is called "Lissamphibia." Two groups developed from the Lissamphibians: Gymnophiona and Batrachia.

The first fossils of Gymnophiona, also called "caecilians," were found in the Lower Jurassic in Arizona. Caecilians are long, slender, legless amphibians. They are globally uncommon. Slightly over 150 species are known today.

Batrachia split into two groups: Caudata and Salientia, the latter sometimes called "Proanura." The earliest fossil caudatans are salamanders from the Upper Jurassic in Kazakhstan.

Salientia split into a node and the earliest frog-like organism. Fossils of *Triadobatrachus massinoti* were found in early Triassic rocks on Madagascar. This animal looks more like a shortened salamander than a true frog. It also has a tail. When *Triadobatrachus* was alive, about 230 million years ago,

RELATIONSHIPS OF AMPHIBIANS

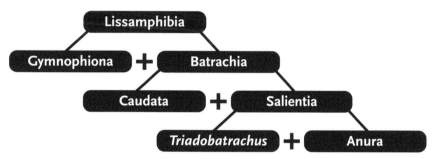

Madagascar was part of Gondwana, which was rifting slowly from south to north between South America and Africa. This split eventually produced the south Atlantic Ocean basin. Early froglike animals were widely distributed during the Triassic. A frog-like amphibian named *Czatkobatrachus*, found in Poland, is only 10 million years younger than *Triadobatrachus* – showing the wide distribution of frog-like animals at this early date.

The other branch from Salientia leads to the node Anura, which means "without a tail." All frogs and toads are descended from this common anuran ancestor.

Fossils of frogs from the early days are rare for two reasons. First, their lightweight bones and skulls are less likely to fossilize than those of heavier-boned animals; and second, frogs inhabit environments such as fast-flowing streams and small ponds. Fossilization is not common in these environments, so fossil frogs are not very commonly found.

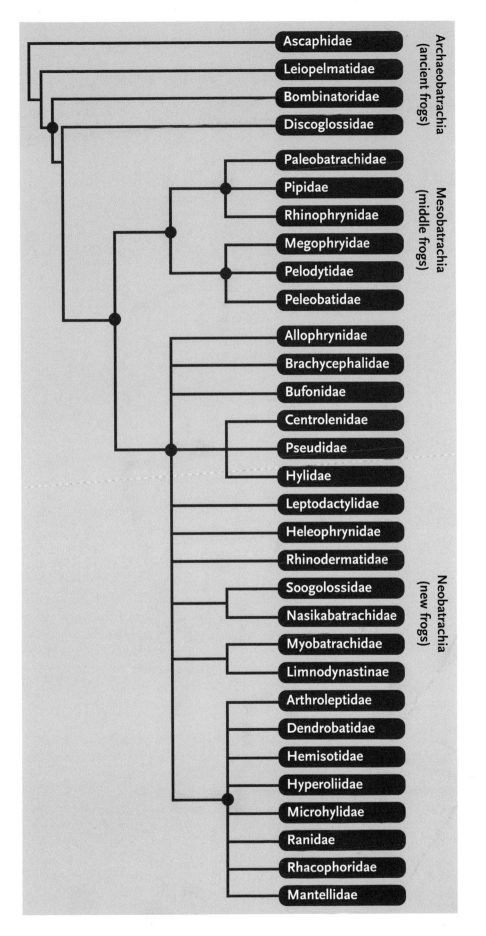

Frog Phylogeny

This frog tree shows the relationship among the 31 frog families.

In an effort to simplify organization of frog groups, many researchers today use a system that divides the living families into three groups:

(1) *Archaeobatrachia* – ancient frogs;
(2) *Mesobatrachia* – middle frogs; and
(3) *Neobatrachia* – new frogs.

↑ Bufonid toads developed when South America and Africa were rifting apart. Over the past 57 million years, one hop at a time, some individuals entered North America, crossed to Siberia and colonized Eurasia and Africa. Others, including ancestors of this South American common toad, *Bufo typhonius*, stayed put.

History of Frogs

FROGS AND TOADS provide one of the greatest success stories on Earth. They have lived on every continent whenever suitable habitat was available. They developed a magnificent and unique form of locomotion – the flying leap. In learning how to hop, their forearms and hind legs developed for propulsion, and to help them absorb the shock of landing. The hip bones elongated, the remaining tail vertebrae fused, the ankle bones grew longer, the spine grew shorter, and the ribs minimized and eventually vanished entirely. And they developed a movable joint, unique to frogs, that lets the pelvis slide up and down the backbone. All these adaptations permit the frog to make, and survive, the explosive leap used to evade capture and catch food.

Frogs and toads also swim differently than either fish or other amphibians, which move from side-to-side. Instead, frogs thrust their legs simultaneously in and then out for propulsion.

Additionally, amphibians developed a tongue, a permeable skin that can be shed or sloughed off, ears to hear the calls produced by their larynx, eyelids and advanced organ systems. Although amphibians need water or moisture for egg-laying and development, they are found high in mountains and in hot deserts – both today and in the fossil record.

The animals that lived and died over immense amounts of time between the early frog-like animals and the first real frogs left no trace that we have been able to find. Paleontologists search the globe looking for fossil animals by finding ancient rocks likely to preserve animals and plants.

Certain layers around the world are well-known preservers of fossil life and are studied by paleontologists and amateurs. Although many smaller fossils are found and studied in a search for dinosaurs or early mammals, only lately has paleontology embraced less charismatic megafauna, like frogs.

The oldest fossil frogs found so far were discovered in Argentina and the southern United States, showing that even in these early days frogs were widely distributed. In the 1960s scientists found *Vieraella herbsti* in early Jurassic sediments in Patagonia, Argentina, dated between 188 and 213 million years old. Another early Jurassic frog, *Prosalirus bitis*, was found in the Kayenta Formation in the Navaho Indian Reservation in Arizona. Therefore, fully recognizable frogs appear in the fossil record before the major dinosaur taxa evolved. North America broke away from Gondwana in the early Jurassic and was fully separated by the middle Jurassic.

The next known fossil frog, *Notobatrachus degiustoi*, was found in sediments from the late Jurassic in Patagonia. It was a relatively large animal, measuring about 6 inches long (15 cm). Recently, frog fossils have been described from the Upper Jurassic Morrison Formation preserved at Dinosaur National Monument, Utah. Two other frog genera of this age were named by O.C. Marsh from specimens collected in the famous Wyoming, South Dakota and Montana "dinosaur wars" of the late 1880s.

Based on only these few specimens, it is impossible to know for sure exactly how these frogs are related to living species. Some taxonomists argue that these early frogs belong on the other side of the anuran node, while others assign them to individual families of primitive frogs.

Because of their Jurassic age, these frogs and some of their descendants are known to have lived before and during the age of dinosaurs. Frogs had ear-bones even in these early days, so it is probable they also evolved the ability to croak, call and trill as well. Their habitats through most of time have been, as they are now, full of plants, insects and the creatures that eat them. Before the end of the Cretaceous, all major orders of animals now present in Earth life had evolved and diversified. The Cretaceous ended about 65 million years ago with the disappearance of the last few species of dinosaurs.

During the Cenozoic, divided into the Tertiary and Quaternary, frogs continued to move around and diversify. Today, they are found on most islands around the world and on all the major continents except Antarctica, which is too cold. Frogs live from the warmest and wettest tropical lowlands to about 17,000 feet above sea level (5,200 m) in the Himalayas. While some areas of Earth have more frogs and frog species than other places, frogs – living from the equator to high latitudes both north and south – are true survivors.

↑ Soft tissues are preserved on this 49-million-year-old fossil of *Messelobatrachus*, found in an open-pit mine near Darmstadt, Germany.

2 Frog Families

CHAPTER TWO

Frog Families

Archaeobatrachia
Ancient frogs

ARCHAEOBATRACHIA IS A COLLECTIVE GROUP, sometimes called "primitive" frogs, with the families Ascaphidae, Leiopelmatidae, Bombinatoridae and Discoglossidae. The ancient frogs are also ancestral to both Mesobatrachia (middle frogs) and Neobatrachia (new frogs).

The so-called primitive frogs do some amazing things and exploit some extraordinary habitats around the world. Fossils of the earliest frogs are surprisingly similar to living members of their groups, showing they probably had similar habits and lifestyles to similar frogs today. Most of the earliest frogs were aquatic, living and looking a lot like the familiar frogs used in science classes and labs, *Pipa* and *Xenopus*.

Frog families have taken fantastic journeys to get to their present-day distribution. They settled wherever they could find a habitat. In each generation, some juveniles remain in the natal pond while others wander. The net effect of this seemingly random movement can result in global migrations over vast amounts of time. Several groups of frogs are used as evidence of the movement of continents over geological time. Some migration pathways opened and closed as the continents shifted around, glaciers grew and melted, and sea level went up and down.

Frogs are found from the Arctic to the tips of South America and Africa; in swamps, in ponds, in streams, on mountains and in deserts worldwide. What started as a tiny hop for a frog has resulted in worldwide distribution for all frog-kind.

← Western toad, *Bufo boreas.*

←← Blue poison frog, *Dendrobates azureus.*

Family *Leiopelmatidae*
New Zealand Frogs

Leiopelmatid frogs are the second oldest group, represented now by only four species in one genus. They are the only native frogs on the islands of New Zealand. They live on mountains where streams and ponds are uncommon. Reproduction is in water, and fertilization is external. They lay around two dozen eggs under damp logs and in crevices. Male frogs of this family take care of the nests. The male Hamilton's frogs, *Leiopelma hamiltoni,* carry their tadpoles on their backs to keep the larvae moist.

The New Zealand government lists Archey's frog, *Leiopelma archeyi,* as near threatened. Hamilton's frog is listed as endangered.

↓ Family Leiopelmatidae. Archey's frog, *Leiopelma archeyi*, New Zealand.

Family *Ascaphidae*
Tailed Frogs

The tailed frog, *Ascaphus truei,* is one of two living members of the ancient family Ascaphidae. Both species live in cold, fast-flowing mountain streams in northwestern North America. Tailed frogs are considered to be among the most primitive of all living frogs because they have nine vertebrae and still have ribs and a tiny muscle to wag their tail.

Tailed frogs do not call, but males find the females anyway. Because of the fast-flowing water, male tailed frogs grasp females tightly during breeding and fertilize them internally. They use a special organ, the "tail," which names the group, to deliver sperm. This adaptation is crucial to survival in their environment because without internal fertilization their sperm would be quickly washed away and lost. Eggs are laid in long strings under cobble-sized rocks in the stream and hatch as tadpoles, which take from one to four years to transform into adults. It takes seven or eight years for a tailed frog to reach sexual maturity.

Most herpetologists have never seen a tailed frog because of the remoteness of the areas in which the animals live and also the cold temperatures at which they are most active. Tailed frogs require permanent streams because the tadpoles take so long to mature. It is assumed that the fossil frogs which so closely resemble the tailed frogs also lived in fast-flowing streams, rather than the shallow pond habitat so commonly associated with frogs and toads today.

Family *Bombinatoridae*
Fire-bellied Toads and Barbourulas

This family is composed of seven species in two genera, *Bombina* and *Barbourula*.

Fire-bellied toads, *Bombina spp.,* live in Europe; across the Bosphorus in parts of Turkey; in far eastern Russia; and in China, Korea and the southern islands of Japan.

Fire-bellied toads are active in daytime and count on their poisonous skin secretions to protect them from predation. Their bright colors are a warning of toxins beneath their pretty skins. Fire-bellied toads also have the "unken reflex"; when frightened, they arch their backs and expose their brightly colored bellies. Male toads can call day and night and can breed up to three times a year. Fire-bellied toads are often used for studies of physiology and embryology and by the pet trade.

The European fire-bellied toad, *Bombina bombina,* breeds all summer. Males can call from underwater, or while floating on the surface. Eggs take two months to hatch to tadpoles, which metamorphose to froglets in the same season they are laid. They were once one of

↓ Family Bombinatoridae. European fire-bellied toad, *Bombina bombina*.

Family *Discoglossidae*
Midwife Toads and Painted Frogs

Fossils of a late Jurassic or early Cretaceous discoglossid frog called *Eodiscoglossus santonje* were found in lithographic limestones at Montsech, Spain. Researchers have also described hundreds of Cretaceous fossil amphibians found in dinosaur beds in Sihetun, in the western part of China's northeastern Liaoning Province, dating from approximately 125 million years ago. One of the fossils is described as a unique discoglossid frog that lived with primitive birds and feathered dinosaurs as well as mammals.

Today, members of this family are found around the coastline of northern Africa and in southwestern Europe. They are divided into two groups, the midwife toads and the painted frogs.

Midwife toads are almost exclusively terrestrial. The common midwife toad is nocturnal and lives in rocky areas, quarries, woodlands and yards. Their days are

the most common amphibians in their habitat. They have declined in some places; in other areas they are still very common. This species inhabits the western end of the family range.

The Oriental fire-bellied toad, *Bombina orientalis*, as the name implies, is the eastern form of this widespread toad. They hibernate from fall through spring, on land or underwater, sometimes in clusters. Breeding is similar to the European form, but female Oriental fire-bellied toads lay about 250 eggs in weekly clutches of approximately 30 eggs, mostly attached to submerged vegetation. Eggs take about two months to hatch. Tadpoles transform before fall.

Barbourulas, *Barbourula spp.*, live in rocky streams and rocky shallow pools in Borneo, Vietnam, the Philippines, Korea and China. They are less known because they hide under the rocks around the edges of the streams and pools and they are camouflaged to match their environments. Barbourulas lay approximately 80 large eggs under stones.

The Philippine aquatic frog, *Barbourula busuangensis*, originally described in 1924, is now considered vulnerable. This frog is fully webbed on both fore and hind limbs, showing its total adaptation to an aquatic lifestyle. It is sensitive to water quality and disappears when streams become polluted.

Another species, *Barbourula kalimantanensis*, is found only in Indonesia and was described in 1978. Some *Barbourula* species seem resistant to human activities; others are habitat dependent and are declining as human activities increase in their landscape.

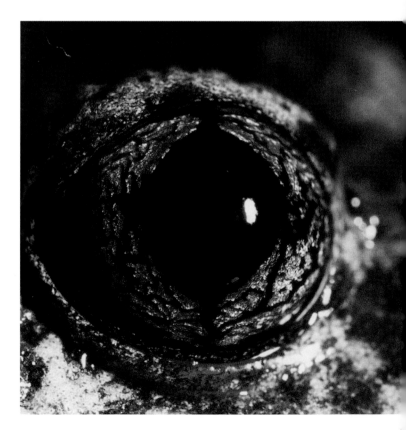

spent in crevices, under logs or in shallow burrows that they excavate with their forelimbs. Mating occurs on land. Males grasp the females, who extrude strings of relatively large eggs. The eggs need to be kept moist during development, so the male midwife toad grabs the egg strings with his feet and wraps them around his hind legs. He carries the eggs for several weeks on his back and legs, rehydrating himself and the egg strings occasionally in water. Just before the eggs hatch, the male puts them in shallow water; hence, the name "midwife toad."

In addition to the common midwife toad, *Alytes obstetricans*, the Iberian midwife toad, *Alytes cisternasii*, inhabits sandy areas in Portugal and Spain. The critically endangered Mallorcan midwife toad, *Alytes muletensis*, lives only on Mallorca in the Spanish Balearic Islands in the Mediterranean. Mallorcan midwife toads were first discovered as fossils and presumed to be extinct until 1980, when they were found and a few were taken into captivity at the Durrell Wildlife Conservation Trust. There they were bred, and captive-born offspring returned to the wild.

Chytrid fungus has been implicated in the disappearance of more than 85 percent of breeding populations of the common midwife toad in Spain (see Chapter 4, Environment & Adaptation). The Israel painted frog, *Discoglossus nigriventer*, was last seen in the wild in the mid 1950s. Draining of its marshy habitat for agriculture has been blamed for its extinction.

← Family Discoglossidae. The eye of the common midwife toad, *Alytes obstetricans*, has vertical elliptical pupils. All other midwife toads, like the Iberian midwife toad, *Alytes cisternasii*, have triangular pupils.

Mesobatrachia
Middle Frogs

The Mesobatrachia are divided into two groups, the Paleobatrachidae and the Pipoidea.

Family *Paleobatrachidae*
Extinct

The Paleobatrachidae are the only known family of frogs that has gone extinct. Fossil Paleobatrachians are found from the upper Jurassic in Europe and the upper Cretaceous in North America. They persisted in both places until quite recently in the Pleistocene.

One genus, *Neusibatrachus*, with two species is known from Jurassic–Cretaceous boundary rocks in Spain and much later in the Miocene in Czechoslovakia. Just a few small anatomical changes separate Paleobatrachians from their near relatives, the Pipoids.

Pipoidea — Pipoid Frogs

Pipoid frogs were widely distributed in the Cretaceous; fossils have been found in Israel, South America and Africa as well as in the Lance Formation of Wyoming and Montana. Pipoids are fully aquatic frogs, with adaptations for bottom feeding and upward-gazing eyes that help them watch out for predators. Their limbs cannot support them on land, although they can move from water to water by paddling across land.

There are two kinds of Pipoid frogs, members of the families Pipidae and Rhinophrynidae.

↑ Family Pipidae. An albino clawed frog, *Xenopus spp.*, with black keratinized claws.

↓ Family Pipidae. Female clawed frogs, *Xenopus laevis*, are larger than males.

Family *Pipidae*
Pipid Frogs

Before 1900, pipid frogs lived only in South America and Africa. They were divided into two subfamilies by the breakup of Gondwana (see page 21). Pipinae lived in South America, and Xenopinidae in Africa.

Like the extinct Paleobatrachians, Pipids are fully aquatic. They have large webbed feet and inward-set forelimbs, and most have fish-like lateral-line organs, which look like lines of white stitches or dots in *Xenopus* skin. They have small eyes with small or no eyelids set well back on the head.

Surinam toads, *Pipa pipa,* have elaborate underwater courtship dances prior to laying the eggs. The male uses his webbed hind feet to sweep the eggs up and onto the female's back. There they imbed in the special pockets in her back skin where the eggs hatch directly into froglets. Other species, like *Pipa carvalhoi*, have a tadpole phase before metamorphosis. Pipid tadpoles are filter feeders; they hover in the middle of the water with their heads pointed down about 45 degrees, and they wriggle while they feed. In their South American habitat, they share tropical waters with predatory fish like piranha. They eat small fish or invertebrates by shoving them whole into their mouths.

While South American Pipids have soft fingertips, keratinized "claws" tip the digits of African *Xenopus spp.*; hence, their common name, "clawed frogs." There are several species of *Xenopus*. Some clawed frogs have more than one set of chromosomes and are called polyploid.

Clawed frogs have courtship rituals and deposit their eggs on the surface of the water. Like most pipids living in sub-Saharan Africa, *Xenopus* lay small eggs in water. These soon hatch into filter-feeding tadpoles. Adult *Xenopus* retain the lateral-line organ, which alerts the frogs to vibrations in the water.

During the 20th century, the African clawed frog, *Xenopus laevis*, was widely used in laboratories as a pregnancy indicator. Since 1940, *Xenopus* has expanded its range to new continents as a result of releases or escapes from captivity. They are still widely used in medical research because their life cycle is so well known and they are so easy to breed. Recently, *Xenopus* has been found to be an asymptomatic carrier of chytrid fungus.

Family *Rhinophrynidae*
Burrowing Toads

The family Rhinophrynidae has only one genus, containing one extinct species and one living species. The Mexican burrowing toad, *Rhinophrynus dorsalis*, lives between Costa Rica and the Rio Grande. As their name suggests, these toads burrow by using their specially adapted hind legs. They spend most of their lives underground, coming out only after heavy rains. Males call from temporary ponds where they meet and clasp females. Fertilization is external and the females lay egg masses. Later the eggs float up to the top one by one. The tadpoles filter feed and tend to congregate in schools before metamorphosis. Mexican burrowing toads have a unique catapult tongue that they use to catch food.

→ **Family Rhinophrynidae. Mexican burrowing toad, *Rhinophrynus dorsalis*.**

Pelobatoidea – Asian Toadfrogs, Parsley Frogs and Spadefoot Toads

Pelobatoid frogs are considered primitive, but transitional. Fossil Pelobatoids have been found in late Cretaceous sediments in Asia and North America. Their descendants are divided into three families: the Megophryidae, the Pelodytidae and the Pelobatidae. In addition to all their other similarities and relationships, all three groups share a common feature: their pupils are vertical.

Family *Megophryidae*
Asian Toadfrogs

More than 100 species in eleven genera of Asian toadfrogs live across Asia and are found in tropical lowland forests of Pakistan and China all the way to the Himalayan mountains. They also occur on many islands of the Philippines, Indonesia, and the Malay Archipelago.

Asian toadfrogs look like leaves in both color and body shape. They also have pointed projections above their eyes that make them look even less like frogs and more like dead leaves. Breeding males rather destroy this illusion; their call is described as a loud repeated clanking. Their tadpoles prefer still waters. They have large upturned mouths and feed at the surface until they begin to transform into adulthood.

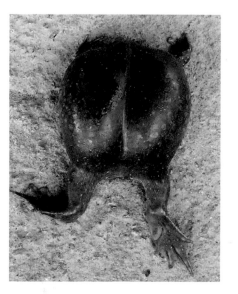

← Family Megophryidae. Malayan horned frog, *Megophrys nasuta*, Sabah, Borneo.

The Malayan horned frog, *Megophrys nasuta,* is described as a ferocious predator on small rodents, lizards, other frogs, spiders, crabs and scorpions. Eggs are laid attached to the undersides of rocks. The tadpoles have large funnel-shaped mouths with which they cling to the underside of the surface; their bodies hang vertically below. They eat small invertebrates and microorganisms at the water's surface.

Scutiger spp. live mostly terrestrial lifestyles as high as 17,000 feet (5,200 m). They breed in cold mountain streams. Males have developed spiny patches on their chests as well as the more usual spiny fingertips to help hold onto the females in the fast-flowing environment.

Family *Pelodytidae*
Parsley Frogs

Fossils of parsley frogs are known from the middle Eocene (approximately 47 million years ago) in Europe. Another fossil was found in North America that dated to the middle Miocene (approximately 15 million years ago), but the family is now extinct in the New World.

Today this family has only two species in one genus,

→ Family Pelodytidae. Common parsley frog, *Pelodytes punctatus,* southern Europe.

Pelodytes. One species is found between the Black and Caspian seas, the other in Europe. They are less than 2 inches (50 mm) long and have longer legs than other Pelobatoids. Parsley frogs look rather like parsley leaves in color; it is to this they owe their name.

Parsley frogs are hard to find except in breeding season. Females can lay up to an astonishing 1,000 eggs, although 100 to 300 is more common. Males call from in the water; females have been reported calling back when they accept the male in amplexus. Tadpoles hatch according to when they were laid; early spring eggs will hatch the same year; fall eggs overwinter and hatch the following spring.

Family *Pelobatidae*
Spadefoot Toads

Today, 10 species in three genera of spadefoot toads live in North America, Central Asia and trans-Caucasia, ranging into Europe with a disjunct in France and another along the south of France and Spain. The family crossed the Straits of Gibraltar and occurs in a tiny part of North Africa on the Atlantic side.

Spadefoots prefer dry areas and sandy soils. They have a spade on their hind feet which they use for burrowing. They sleep during the day, are active in the cooler night and can hide in deep burrows for a long time during droughts. They are a sit-and-wait predator, moving around only during breeding season.

A chorus of calling males can be heard up to a mile away. Males may compete for females, and some are injured in the struggle. Females lay eggs in temporary ponds for only a couple of days. The eggs hatch quickly. American spadefoots transform into froglets in around three weeks; Europeans take longer, and some even have to overwinter as a tadpole.

The earliest fossils of spadefoot toads date from the Tertiary. The first known *Scaphiopus* fossils are from North America, from about 35 million years ago. The earliest *Pelobates* fossils are from Europe, from about 47 million years ago, suggesting an Old World origin for the New World toads.

The European common spadefoot, *Pelobates fuscus*, prefers sandy soil to burrow and breeds in temporary pools and ditches.

↑ Family Pelobatidae. An Eastern spadefoot toad, *Scaphiopus holbrookii*, just after metamorphosis is small enough to fit on a penny, but will grow larger if it survives.

In North America, the Eastern spadefoot, *Scaphiopus holbrookii*, and plains spadefoot, *Spea bombifrons*, live from Southern Mexico to southern Canada, growing up to 4 inches (100 mm). Both have a digging tubercle on the hind feet, which gives rise to the name "spadefoot." They can live in deserts because they can dig their own burrows. When the rains fall, they congregate at temporary pools to breed. It takes the eggs two weeks to hatch into tadpoles. At this point, more rain is needed; otherwise, the ponds dry up and the plant-eating tadpoles die. Some tadpoles become cannibalistic under these harsh conditions, permitting some individuals to survive long enough to transform into frogs by eating the bodies of their herbivorous relatives.

↑ Family Microhylidae. Asian painted frog, *Kaloula pulchra*, southeastern Asia.

↓ Family Brachycephalidae. The Karin Hills frog, *Brachytarsophrys carinensis*, lives in southern Myanmar, northern Thailand and the mountains of southern China.

Neobatrachia
New Frogs

The Neobatrachia include 95 percent of the known species of frogs. There are 20 families of Neobatrachians divided into the "Bufonids" and the Ranoidea.

"Bufonids," aka "Hyloids"

Bufonids is a catchall term for several frog families; there is no evidence to show that they arose from a single ancestor. This history results in confusing answers to the familiar question, "What's the difference between 'frogs' and 'toads'?" Because toads descended from different ancestors, just like the frogs did, they have many different adaptations within the general category of being "toad-like."

Family *Allophrynidae*
Ruthven's Frogs

Ruthven's frog, *Allophryne ruthveni*, is the only living species in this family. They live in trees in tropical rainforests in northeastern South America. It is known that they breed in temporary ponds formed by heavy rains. Their tadpoles are still undescribed.

Family *Brachycephalidae*
Three-toed Toadlets

There are two genera and three species of three-toed toadlets; all are terrestrial in rainforests in southeastern Brazil. This family is occasionally called the "Gold frog family," after its most brightly colored members. Whatever their common name, they lay eggs on land which hatch directly into froglets.

The gold frog, *Brachycephalus ephippium,* has a bright yellow body. Photographs of this species are particularly arresting when they show the breeding pair, or an aggregation. The other genus in this family is named *Psyllophryne* and has a similar lifestyle to its nearest relative.

The smallest frog in the Southern Hemisphere is reported to be the Brazilian gold frog *Brachycephalus didactylus*. It measures about ⅜ of an inch (9.5 mm) from snout to vent. It is nearly exactly the same size as the smallest frog in the Northern Hemisphere, *Eleutherodactylus iberia*. Both frogs are tied for the title of "world's smallest tetrapod."

↓ Family Brachycephalidae. Two gold frogs, *Brachycephalus ephippium,* on a leaf in the Atlantic rainforest.

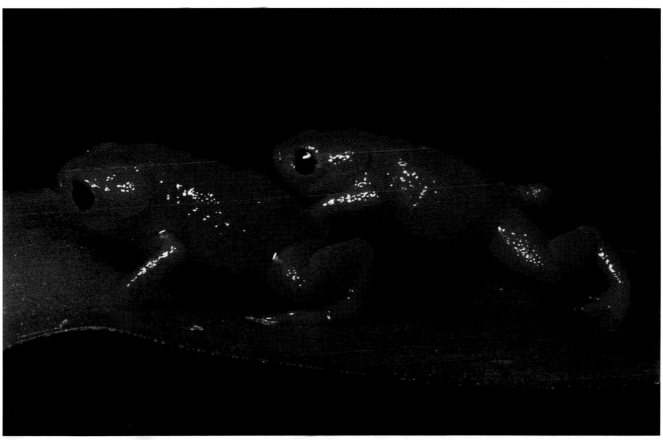

↑ Family Bufonidae. The marine toad, *Bufo marinus*, is native to the Atlantic side of the New World and was introduced worldwide. They have become a scourge in Australia, devouring or poisoning other wildlife.

↓ Family Bufonidae. Natterjack toad, *Bufo calamita*, Europe.

Family *Bufonidae*
True Toads, Harlequin Frogs and Others

More than half of the nearly 400 known species in this family belong to one widely distributed genus, *Bufo*. The earliest fossils of recognizable Bufonids date from about 57 million years ago along the rapidly rifting line between South America and Africa. From the South American side, they invaded North America, crossed into Siberia and have proceeded to colonize Eurasia and Africa since then.

Today, they are found on all the continents except Antarctica and Australia. Wherever they are, they all look similar. They are short-legged, heavy animals with warty glands on their legs and bodies and a large parotoid gland aft of their eyes. They also have no teeth, although this is not a feature likely to be observable in life. A toad's eyes are shifted rather farther forward than a frog's.

↑ **Family Bufonidae. The extremely toxic Colorado River toad, *Bufo alvarius*.**

As many children discover, toads are much calmer animals and are easier to catch than frogs. Toads barely even leap. Instead, a toad is more likely to urinate on its surprised captor and escape in the spray of its own moisture. Truly annoyed toads will release toxins from their parotoid glands, which contain a chemistry set of foul-smelling fluids and toxins.

Ingestion of toxins from the Colorado River toad, *Bufo alvarius*, can be fatal to dogs. Anyone handling any toad should wash as soon as possible and avoid touching their eyes or other parts of the body until clean.

Toads lay astonishing numbers of eggs in long paired strings. A 3-inch-long (76 mm) toad can lay 20,000 or more eggs, which take only a day or two to develop into tadpoles. Toads often lay eggs in ephemeral waters like tire ruts and water bowls, and their newly metamorphosing young can seem like an invading army. Toads eat an astonishing array and number of invertebrates. A study of urban toads in the early 1900s found they ate more than 1,000 bugs, mostly ants, a day. As their food was destroyed by petrochemicals and insecticides from the 1950s onward, toads have disappeared from many cities and suburban areas.

Frog or Toad? Some General Differences

Frogs	Toads
• long and skinny	• short and stubby
• long legs and arms	• short legs and arms
• longer faces	• blunt faces
• eyes that see up and over to their butts	• eyes that see mainly forward with a little periphery
• smooth skin	• warty skin
• not too many wrinkles at joints	• sometimes very saggy, baggy skin
• not as successful at tongue hunting	• extremely successful at tongue hunting – implies better brain power and better resolution on eyesight
• "dignified" mating, lay mostly egg masses	• massive frothy free-for-alls ending in amplexed pairs stuck for days laying eggs in strings
• slower-developing tadpoles	• very fast-developing tadpoles
• lower temperatures and moister places	• higher temperatures and drier places
• most frog species have five toes, jointed 2-2-3-4-3	• some true toads (and a few frogs) have only four toes on their hind feet

↑ Family Bufonidae. A pink-bellied harlequin frog, *Atelopus flavescens,* French Guiana and Brazil.

The marine toad, *Bufo marinus,* was introduced into Australia in the early 20th century. It was incorrectly believed that *marinus* would eat the sugar cane beetles that were infesting the fields. It didn't. But it began a one-species invasion of the isolated continent and is now considered a major problem. The species is spreading rapidly and eating everything in its path. Administrators are proposing toadproof fences to keep the invaders from spreading into other areas. Marine toads are also commonly called "giant toads" and, specifically in Australia, "cane toads." They can grow up to 10 inches (250 mm) long.

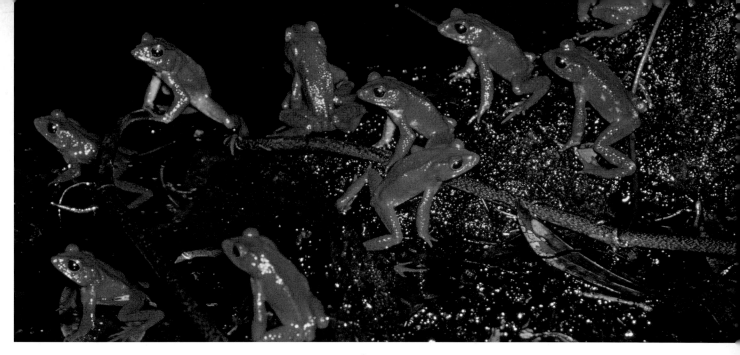

Natterjack toads, *Bufo calamita,* live in Europe and in the United Kingdom. Eggs are laid from May through September, but in single strings rather than the double string more common in other toad species. It is an offense to harm or kill natterjacks in the United Kingdom.

The golden toad, *Bufo periglenes,* was known only from the nearly pristine Monteverde Cloud Forest Reserve in Costa Rica. Photographs of the tiny bright orange frogs captured the imagination of ecotourists, herpetologists and photographers, many of whom visited during the few days of the year when the toads would swarm out to mate in great congregations. The last one was seen in the late 1980s, and the cause of their disappearance is unknown.

The European common toad, *Bufo bufo,* is a species known to the Romans and from which the word "buffoon" comes. They lay eggs communally. The laying of multiple egg masses in the same place can raise the water temperature and provide individual eggs with some protection from predators.

Harlequin frogs, *Atelopus spp.,* are found in Central and South America. They are brightly colored and have potent toxins. *Atelopus oxyrhynchus* holds the world record for two frogs in amplexus at 125 days.

The West African live-bearing toad, *Nectophrynoides occidentalis,* has internal fertilization of only a few eggs and gives birth to metamorphosed froglets. Slender toads, *Ansonia spp.,* of Southeast Asia, like the earliest frogs, breed in torrential cascades and swift-flowing streams. Their eggs are laid in strings and hatch into tadpoles with specially adapted mouths that stick to rocks.

↑ Family Bufonidae. Dozens of photographs are available of golden toads, *Bufo periglenes,* and for several years there were rumors that some had been taken into captivity in Europe or Japan and were being bred. As time passes, however, the photographs seem to be all that remains of this exquisite amphibian.

↓ Family Bufonidae. The European common toad, *Bufo bufo,* hunting a moth.

↑ Family Centrolenidae. Fleischmann's glass frog, *Hyalinobatrachium fleischmanni*, Belize.

Family *Centrolenidae*
Glass Frogs

Glass frogs are active at night in trees in damp forests, usually on the slopes of mountains in South and Central America.

The three genera in this family, *Centrolene, Cochranella,* and *Hyalinobatrachium,* collectively have slightly more than 100 species. The group gets its common name, "glass frogs," from the transparent belly skin shared by all of its members. They are all tiny. The largest ones are 3 inches long (76 mm), but most are less than 1 inch (25 mm).

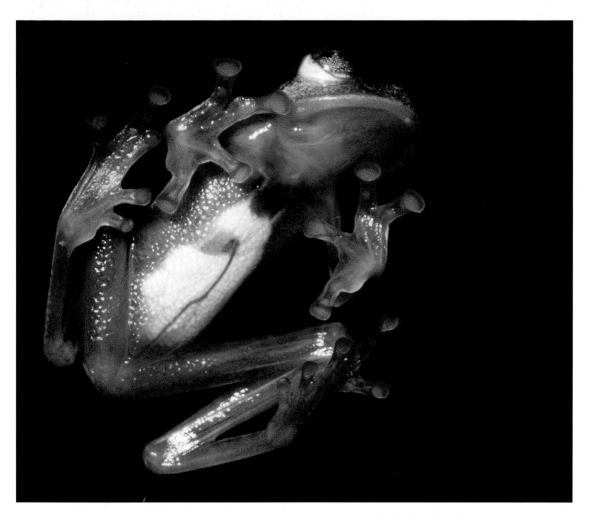

↑ Family Centrolenidae. Bare-hearted glass frog, *Hyalinobatrachium colymbiphyllum,* cloud forests of Costa Rica.

Because of the transparency of their skin, glass frogs have been used for teaching purposes. The belly skin of several glass frogs, including *Hyalinobatrachium vireovittatum,* is so transparent that the internal organs can be seen through the skin.

Glass frogs lay small clutches of eggs on the male's territorial leaf above streams. Male parents usually watch over the eggs, sometimes perching on them. When the eggs hatch, the tadpoles drop into the water and swim away. Blue-spined glass frogs, *Centrolene prosoblepon,* have territorial fights prior to breeding. The bony hooks under the male's arms are used for fighting. These frogs live in Costa Rica.

→ Family Centrolenidae. La Palma glass frog, *Hyalinobatrachium valerioi.*

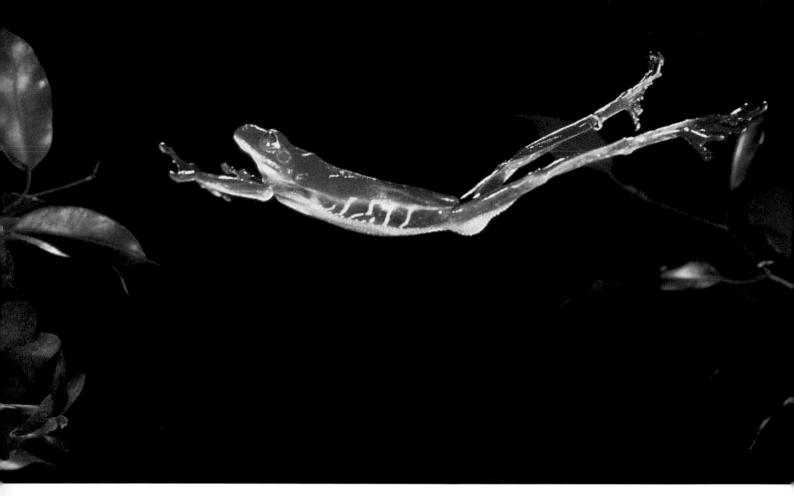

↑ Family Hylidae. Red-eyed treefrog, *Agalychnis callidryas*, leaping.

Family *Pseudidae*
Paradox Frogs

The handful of species in two genera of Paradox frogs are nocturnal and aquatic; they live in permanent water in tropical lowlands mostly east of the Andes in South America. They breed in water, fertilize externally, and lay eggs which hatch to free-swimming tadpoles.

Paradox frogs, *Pseudis paradoxa*, float around at the surface of the water and have highly webbed digits that show how fully aquatic they are. Eggs are laid in water and hatch into tadpoles, which grow to an incredible four times the size of the adults. Tadpoles can reach 9 inches (230 mm) before transforming into adults, which are only about one to two inches long (25–50 mm). The huge loss of size from tadpole to adult is the paradox from which the family gets its name. The large tadpoles are reportedly eaten as delicacies by local people. The other genus of Paradox frogs, *Lysapus,* has two species. Both are smaller than *Pseudis paradoxa*.

↓ Family Pseudidae. Paradox frog, *Pseudis paradoxa*, South America.

← Family Hylidae.
Red-eyed treefrog,
*Agalychnis
callidryas*, gliding.

Family *Hylidae*
Amero-Australian Treefrogs

The approximately 775 species in 40 genera of tree-frogs in this group are mostly tree dwelling and nocturnal. Many are bright green with flashy colors along the sides.

Hylids are widespread in the New World; they live from Canada to Argentina. They occur in Tasmania, Australia and New Guinea, as well as parts of south-eastern Asia and northern China; all of Korea and Japan as well as around the Black Sea; throughout Europe; and in a thin band along the Mediterranean coast of Africa. Fossil Hylids have been found in South America, dating from more than 57 million years ago.

Treefrogs have large, round adhesive disks at the ends of their fingers; the frogs use them to climb and hold onto vegetation, rocks and humanmade objects.

→ Family Hylidae. Hourglass treefrog,
Hyla ebraccata, central and northern
South America.

↑ Family Hylidae. Pacific treefrog, *Pseudacris regilla*, western North America.

← Family Hylidae. Casque-headed treefrog, *Hemiphractus proboscideus*, Ecuador.

↓ Family Hylidae. A trio of red-eyed treefrogs, *Agalychnis callidryas*, tropical New World.

Casque-headed treefrogs include *Trachycephalus spp.,* found in Pacific lowlands from Colombia to Peru and Eastern Brazil. The Ecuadorian casque-headed frog, *Hemiphractus proboscideus,* looks like a dead leaf and is entirely terrestrial. Males carry fertilized eggs on their back; the young frogs develop directly and hatch out as froglets. The United States has one member of this group – the lowland burrowing treefrog, *Pternohyla fodiens.*

Chorus frogs, *Pseudacris spp.,* include the Pacific treefrog, *Pseudacris regilla,* the "ribbet frog" known to every movie fan. At some time in the early days of talkies, someone recorded frogs in a pond, probably in Griffith Park near the famous Hollywood sign. The same audio loop is used over and over in movies, leading to hysteria among amphibian researchers who hear "ribbet" in darkest Africa, South America and Australia – and on outer space planets. The Pacific treefrog is actually restricted to the western edge of North America.

↑ **Family Hylidae. Tiger-striped leaf frog,** *Phyllomedusa tomopterna,* **Amazon Basin.**

↓ **Family Hylidae. Marsupial frog,** *Gastrotheca ovifera,* **with froglets in pouch, Venezuela.**

↑ Family Hylidae. Pygmy marsupial frog, *Flectonotus pygmaeus*, with eggs on its back, Andean South America.

↓ Family Hylidae. The common water-holding frog, *Cyclorana platycephala*, lives in arid interior areas in Australia.

Leaf frogs, *Agalychnis spp., Phyllomedusa spp.* and others, were named because of their uncanny resemblance to leaves. Most members of the genus have the long skinny legs characteristic of a good jumper. Treefrogs need to be good jumpers and good landers, although it is easier for them to walk along branches and climb trunks. The ubiquitous red-eyed treefrog, *Agalychnis callidryas,* is a member of this group.

Marsupial frogs, *Flectonotus* and *Gastrotheca,* are so called because the females carry their eggs on their backs or in pouches on their bellies, where the eggs are surrounded by gills that assist in oxygen transport. In back-carrying marsupial frogs, froglets emerge from the egg. At higher elevations, females carry the newly hatched tadpoles to water. There the tadpoles finish their growth and transform into frogs. *Flectonotus spp.* eggs are deposited in water-filled cavities or bromeliad leaves. They hatch into tadpoles, which don't eat but finish their metamorphosis and emerge as froglets.

↑ Family Hylidae. Blacksmith treefrog, *Hyla faber*, South America.

The Map treefrog, *Hyla geographica*, lives on the island of Trinidad. Its tadpoles live in shoals. Sometimes they swim together and stir up food-bearing sediment from the bottom; other times they seek safety from predators as a group.

Northern cricket frogs, *Acris crepitans*, are variably colored small frogs that were more widely distributed in the North-central U.S. states until the middle 1980s, when they went into a much-studied but still mysterious decline. Recently, pesticides have been implicated in their decline.

Blacksmith treefrogs, *Hyla faber*, engage in combat during the breeding season; hence their popular name, gladiator treefrogs.

↑ Family Leptodactylidae. The symbol of Puerto Rico, *Eleutherodactylus coqui*, called the coqui frog for its loud and piercing call, is beloved on its home island but loathed in Hawaii, where it was accidentally introduced.

↓ Family Leptodactylidae. Argentine horned frog, *Ceratophrys ornata*, South America.

Family *Leptodactylidae*
Leptodactylid Frogs

Leptodactylids are the largest family in the "Bufonid" group, with approximately 850 species in about 50 genera. The oldest fossil of the group was found in South American rocks dating to about 65 million years ago. Not as old, but amazingly well preserved, is a whole specimen in amber from the Dominican Republic in the Caribbean from about 37 million years ago.

Most Leptodactylids live in South and Central America, the Caribbean Islands and Mexico, while only six species are found in the southern United States. They occupy every habitat, from moist montane down to dry deserts and tropical lowlands.

Many male Leptodactylids whip up foam nests for the eggs, which may be laid and develop in a variety of environments from water to moist places on land.

The genus *Eleutherodactylus* contains more than 600 species. One species, the Puerto Rican live-bearing frog, *Eleutherodactylus jasperi,* was discovered in 1976.

This frog, now thought to be extinct, had internal fertilization and gave birth to live froglets in ponded water in bromeliad plants in mountain forests on Puerto Rico. The species was last seen in the wild in the early 1980s. All the other *Eleutherodactylus spp.* have direct-developing eggs, where metamorphosis occurs within the egg. When the eggs hatch, small froglets emerge.

The symbol of Puerto Rico, *Eleutherodactylus coqui,* called the coqui frog, and its cousin, the greenhouse frog, *Eleutherodactylus planirostris,* apparently moved from their home island halfway around the world to the state of Hawaii. While beloved on Puerto Rico, loud coquis and inoffensive greenhouse frogs are hated in Hawaii, where state officials have tried eradication methods including steam, citrus or caffeine sprays and other control methods. The frogs apparently arrived and then spread on greenhouse plants, which, considering the creatures' lifestyle, makes sense. Males nest in dead leaves or other plant debris and guard the egg clutches. There is no tadpole phase; tiny froglets hatch from the eggs after direct development. Males also rehydrate the eggs and stay with the newly metamorphosed froglets for a few days. Coquis and greenhouse frogs have also naturalized in the Virgin Islands and in Louisiana and Florida on the U.S. mainland.

↑ Family Leptodactylidae. Common Coqui, *Eleutherodactylus coqui,* parachuting from a tree, Puerto Rico.

↓ Family Leptodactylidae. Froglets in eggs. Costa Rica.

↑ Family Leptodactylidae. Discovered in Cuba, *Eleutherodactylus iberia* is tied for the title of "world's smallest frog."

↓ Family Leptodactylidae. Titicaca water frog, *Telmatobius culeus*, Peru.

The smallest frog in the Northern Hemisphere was discovered in 1996 in Monte Iberia, Cuba, in leaf litter in a humid rainforest. The frog is so small that three could fit in the space taken up by its scientific name *Eleutherodactylus iberia* (as it appears here). At ⅜ inch (9.5 mm), it is tied for the title of "world's smallest frog" with the Brazilian gold frog, *Brachycephalus didactylus*. Both frogs are also tied for the title of "world's smallest tetrapod."

↑ Family Rhinodermatidae. Darwin's frog, *Rhinoderma darwinii*, and froglet just released from his father's vocal sac.

← Family Heleophrynidae. Natal ghost frog, *Heleophryne natalensis*, South Africa.

Family *Heleophrynidae*
Ghost Frogs

The five known species of ghost frogs are all members of the genus *Heleophryne* and live in southernmost Africa in rocky fast-flowing streams. They all have vertical pupils and are normally colored. The name "ghost frog" may derive from the original specimens coming from Cape Town's Skeleton Gorge, rather than from any color or unusual appearance in life. Ghost frogs use their sticky finger pads to climb wet slippery rocks.

Males have extra flaps of skin and spines on their body surfaces which help them hold the slightly larger females during breeding. Large eggs are deposited in the water under rocks, in pools or on the edges of streams. The tadpoles swim against the current and use their huge suction-disk mouths to hold on in the flowing water. They are algae grazers by day; at night they climb rocks with their mouths. It takes the tadpoles more than a year to transform into adult frogs.

Hewitt's ghost frog, *Heleophryne hewitti*, is listed as endangered by the government of South Africa, and the Table Mountain ghost frog, *Heleophryne rosei*, is listed as vulnerable. The Cape ghost frog, *Heleophryne purcelli*, lives only in the mountain streams of far southern Africa.

Family *Rhinodermatidae*
Mouth-brooding Frogs

Frogs in this family are limited to one genus, which lives in temperate rainforests in southern South America along the Pacific edge. There are two species; each lays about 20 eggs on land, where they are attended by the males for nearly three weeks. Hatching tadpoles are taken up into the males' mouths. After that each species has its own breeding strategy. Male *Rhinoderma rufium* frogs carry hatching tadpoles to water, while tadpoles of *Rhinoderma darwinii* continue growing into froglets in their fathers' vocal sacs.

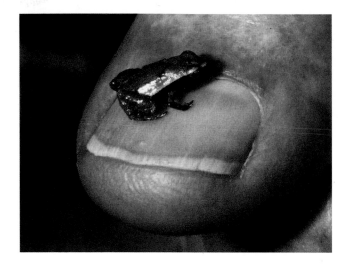

← Family Sooglossidae. The Seychelles frog, *Sooglossus gardineri*, is one of the world's smallest frogs. This is a full-grown male.

Family *Nasikabatrachidae*
Purple Frogs

The announcement of a new family of frogs in the Western Ghats of India in October 2003 made front-page news around the world. Discovering new species is not uncommon, but discovering a new family of vertebrate is considered an exceptional event.

Purple frogs were discovered while a well was being dug in a cardamom plantation. Villagers gave the odd purple creature to Dr. S.D. Beju, who was studying plants in the area. The describers of the Kerala purple frog, *Nasikabatrachus sahyadrensis,* suggest the species remained unknown for so long because it is only surface active for two weeks each year. The other 50 weeks, purple frogs live underground, burrowing with their stout forelimbs and reinforced snout.

Only a few observations of breeding have been made so far, and all have been during the monsoon – when for two weeks of the year purple frogs emerge to reproduce. Males, smaller than females, clasp, breed and vanish. Little more is known so far, but studies continue into all aspects of their lifestyle. DNA analysis showed that purple frogs are more closely related to *Sooglossidae* from the Seychelles, then to frogs from Africa. How the frogs are related contributes to plate tectonic theory by showing that India and the Seychelles were once attached to Africa, and that, until recently, at least some parts of India have remained relatively isolated.

Family *Sooglossidae*
Seychelles Frogs

The Seychelles are a granitic fragment of Gondwana that is currently northeast of Madagascar. Two genera of frogs are found there, *Neomantis* and *Sooglossus*. They live an almost exclusively terrestrial lifestyle, even depositing eggs on land, where they are attended by their mothers. Two reproductive styles are followed: one where froglets hatch from eggs, the other where nonfeeding tadpoles ride on the mothers' backs until they metamorphose. All three species are vulnerable as human population and development increase on the Seychelles.

Family *Myobatrachidae*
Australian Toadlets and Water frogs

All members of this group live in New Guinea, Australia and Tasmania. The first fossils are known from the mid-Tertiary in Australia, about 15 to 25 million years ago. Myobatrachids are survivors in Australia's most arid habitats. Many are burrowers, and most have spades on their hind feet for digging. Females whip up foam nests for eggs, in burrows filled with water, in open water or on land. Almost 10 percent of the species in this family are endangered, and about 5 percent are considered vulnerable. All species are brightly colored on the belly, and some are colorful on the back as well.

↓ Family Nasikabatrachidae. Kerala purple frog, *Nasikabatrachus sahyadrensis*, India.

Male Bibron's toadlets, *Pseudophryne bibronii,* sit next to clutches of eggs laid in damp holes under stones. The eggs hatch as soon as rains provide the necessary moisture before each tadpole can swim away. The eggs may have to wait up to 90 days to hatch in especially dry conditions.

Two unusual southwestern Australian species, the sandhill frog, *Arenophryne rotunda,* and the turtle frog, *Myobatrachus gouldii,* burrow head first and lay eggs up to 3 feet deep (1 m) in moist sand. The eggs develop directly and hatch as fully formed froglets.

The pouched frog, *Assa darlingtoni,* lays eggs right on the ground. When the tadpoles hatch, they wriggle into special pouches on the male and develop directly into frogs over the next two months.

Two species of gastric-brooding frogs, *Rheobatrachus silus* and *Rheobatrachus vitellinus,* were described. They bred in fast-flowing streams. The females swallowed the tadpoles, which grew into froglets in their stomachs. *Rheobatrachus silus* was last seen in the early 1980s; both species are believed to be extinct.

↑ Family Limnodynastinae. The banjo frog, *Limnodynastes dumerilii*, is sometimes called a pobblebonk.

↓ Family Limnodynastinae. The crucifix toad, *Notaden bennettii*, lives in NSW and Queensland, Australia.

Family *Limnodynastinae*
Australian Ground Frogs

The approximately 50 species in 11 genera of Limno-dynastid frogs live in New Guinea, Australia and Tasmania. They live either underground or at the surface in deserts, grasslands and rainforests. Some burrow down with sharp spade-like tubercles and survive harsh desert conditions by storing water in their bodies. Aboriginal Australians dug up these large frogs and forced out their stored water when in desperate need of a drink.

The Australian banjo frog, *Limnodynastes dumerilii*, lives in marshes and swamps, but avoids flowing creeks. The common name comes from the sound of the call, which is described as resembling the "plonk" of a banjo.

The Australian desert spadefoot toad, *Notaden nichollsi*, lives in the driest parts of northern Australia. It, like many species of Australian frogs, holds water, but is not used by Aboriginal people because it is small and it releases a smelly skin secretion when bothered. The thick white fluid dries to an elastic film.

Ranoidea — Ranoid Frogs

Ranid frogs are most diverse in the Old World. Their center of diversity is in Africa, but their path to the New World was by way of Asia and the Bering land bridge. They reached the Western Hemisphere in the Oligocene.

Family *Arthroleptidae*
Squeakers and Cricket Frogs

Squeakers and cricket frogs are found in a wide range of forest habitats – including wet mountain forests and rainforests – in sub-Saharan Africa. There are about 75 species in eight known genera. Most members of this family lay eggs in water and have tadpoles. A few genera, including *Arthroleptis* and *Coracodichus,* lay a few large eggs on land which develop directly and hatch as froglets.

Tiny common squeakers, *Arthroleptis stenodactylus,* live under dead forest leaves from Angola to northeastern South Africa. Males have an elongated third finger and call from under plants and leaves. Eggs are laid on land in damp earth and under decaying leaves. The eggs develop directly and hatch as froglets.

Male hairy frogs, *Trichobatrachus robustus,* have skin extrusions, rather like little hairs, which help them exchange oxygen while they are underwater tending their eggs.

↓ Family Arthroleptidae. Hairy frog, *Trichobatrachus robustus,* Western Africa.

↑ Family Dendrobatidae. A reticulated poison frog, *Dendrobates reticulatus,* carries two tadpoles in the Amazon rainforest of Peru.

Family *Dendrobatidae*
Poison Frogs

The 170 species in nine genera of poison frogs live in rainforests and humid forests centered on the Equator in the top eastern half of South America and parts of Central America.

Brightly colored genera, including *Phyllobates, Epipedobates, Minyobates* and *Dendrobates,* are toxic. Native peoples where these frogs live derived poison for their arrows and blow-gun darts, which they then used to kill larger animals. Fanciers often get into great arguments about whether to call poison frogs "poison arrow frogs" or "poison dart frogs."

↑ Family Dendrobatidae. Green and black poison frog, *Dendrobates auratus*, tropical New World and introduced in Hawaii.

← Family Dendrobatidae. Male Strawberry poison frogs, *Dendrobates pumilio*, wrestle for territory, Central America.

↑ Family Dendrobatidae. Male granular poison frog, *Dendrobates granulifer*, calling in a Costa Rican rainforest.

↓ Family Dendrobatidae. Yellow-banded poison frog, *Dendrobates leucomelas*, northern South America.

Some poison frogs are nearly the smallest frogs in the world; they can measure as little as half an inch long (12.5 mm) when fully grown. Others grow to nearly two inches long (50 mm). Poison frogs are active in the day. That and their vivid coloration make them favorites of frogkeepers and photographers worldwide.

Like some other species on Earth, Dendrobatids get together to breed and fight. Both males and females are aggressive and wrestle. Males chase or attack each other if posturing fails to settle the issue. Poison frog eggs are laid on the ground and watched by either parent. When the eggs hatch, the tadpoles hitch a ride to water on their parents' backs. Some species deposit the tadpoles in bromeliad plants that hold water; others use water-filled cavities; and others use ponds or streams.

Females of some species of *Dendrobates* deposit sterile eggs in bromeliad "ponds" after putting in tadpoles. The sterile eggs nourish the tadpoles – otherwise, they'd starve. This is one of those "which came first, the egg or the tadpole" situations in which nature so abounds.

↑ Family Hemisotidae. Marbled shovel-
nosed frog, *Hemisus marmoratus,* Kenya.

Family *Hemisotidae*
Shovel-nosed Frogs

All eight species in this family belong to one genus, *Hemisus,* and burrow head first in scrub forests and savannas in sub-Saharan Africa. They are burrowers and are rarely seen because they spend almost their entire lives underground.

Males call and grab the females, who begin to dig down, head first, and create an underground chamber for the eggs. Fertilization is external, then the male digs his way out of the chamber. The eggs are guarded by the females in the burrow. When the tadpoles hatch, the female digs a tunnel and either carries or guides the tadpoles out of the burrow and into the water.

Other oddities distinguish individual members of this group. The marbled shovel-nosed frog, *Hemisus marmoratus,* has a prehensile tongue mechanism.

Family *Hyperoliidae*
Reed and Sedge Frogs

The approximately 240 species of reed and sedge frogs are divided into 19 genera, which live in sub-Saharan Africa, Madagascar and the Seychelles. Reed and sedge frogs look rather like treefrogs with long limbs and enlarged finger pads. Their pupils are ellipsoids and they change color depending on environmental factors. They breed and lay eggs in various places, including in cavities on land, in foam nests on plants, or in water. Regardless of where deposited the eggs hatch to free-swimming tadpoles, which become froglets in the water.

A few well-known species include the golden leaf-folding frog, *Afrixalus brachycnemis;* the marbled reed frog, *Hyperolius marmoratus;* the Seychelles Islands treefrog, *Tachycnemis seychellensis;* and the sedge frogs, *Hyperolius viridiflavus.*

The name "leaf-folding frog" refers to the habit of several members of the family that fold leaves around newly laid eggs to prevent desiccation. They lay their eggs on leaves over water; newly hatched tadpoles just fall in. One species, *Hyperolius obstetricans,* lays eggs. Later, frogs, not tadpoles, hatch out of the eggs.

Tadpoles of *Leptopelis spp.* have a tougher escape job than getting out of a leaf. Their parents bury eggs somewhere near water. When it rains, the water overruns the buried eggs, which hatch, and the tadpoles wriggle out and swim away.

The trilling reed frog, *Hyperolius parkeri,* calls with a bird-like warble. Eggs are deposited on flat blades of grass just above the water. Males are larger than females, which is reported to be unique among African treefrogs. The water lily frog, *Hyperolius pusillus,* lays eggs in the spaces where water lily leaves overlap.

← Family Hyperoliidae. Natal forest treefrog, *Leptopelis natalensis,* South Africa.

↑ Family Hyperoliidae. Marbled reed frog, *Hyperolius marmoratus,* enjoying a frog's eye view of its world, eastern and southern Africa.

→ Family Ranidae. Goliath frog, *Conraua goliath*, Cameroon, Africa.

↑ Family Ranidae. African bullfrog, *Pyxicephalus adspersus*, full face, South Africa.

↓ Family Ranidae. African bullfrog, *Pyxicephalus adspersus*, profile.

Family *Ranidae*
True Frogs

There are about 650 species in about 45 genera of Ranid frogs in North America, Central America, northern South America, Africa, except for the Sahara, Europe, Scandinavia, all of conterminous Asia except the far northern tundra, the offshore southeast Asian islands, New Guinea, and the extreme tip of Australia. Ranids are absent from Antarctica, Greenland, Madagascar and New Zealand.

Ranid frogs began their 50-million-year jouney by hopping out of Africa in the Eocene. They crossed Eurasia and entered North America in the Oligocene, crossing the Panamanian land bridge into South America when it became available in the Pliocene. The tropical branch of the family arrived in India during the Oligocene–Miocene and its members have spread through tropical Asia ever since.

At about 50 million years since the Ranids hopped out of Africa, and estimating a ground route distance from Africa to South America at 25,000 miles (40,200 km), these frogs advanced about 32 inches per year (82 cm).

Ranids are still most diverse in Africa, followed by Asia. Europe and the Americas have one genus, *Rana*. They live everywhere: underground, ponds, streams, lakes and rivers, terrestrial habitats and up into trees. They have adapted their body forms to each lifestyle. Ranids can have elongated digits and huge webs for gliding, or toepad-like disks for climbing, or hind-foot webbing for swimming. Most Ranid frogs lay eggs – which become tadpoles – in water. Some lay terrestrial eggs that undergo direct development. One is known that lays a few eggs in moist cavities. The eggs hatch to nonfeeding tadpoles, which finish their development in the nest.

Africa

African bullfrogs, *Pyxicephalus adspersus,* live in a large part of sub-Saharan Africa. Males grow to about 9 inches long (23 cm); females are smaller, about 4 inches long (10 cm). Big ones can weigh around 4.4 pounds (2 kg). They use their strong hind legs to dig burrows and coat themselves in a protective cocoon in which they survive the dry season. When the rains return, the frogs join other animals, including elephants and other large mammals, at watering holes and pools.

Males are territorial and call from clearly defined areas. The call is described as a roar-like bellow. Females lay an astonishing three to four thousand eggs in shallow water. The eggs hatch to fat, heart-shaped tadpoles a mere two days later. Three weeks after the eggs are laid, the tadpoles metamorphose to small frogs and leave the water. Small African bullfrogs eat each other. Their survival to first year in the wild is very low. Adult "Pyxi's" defend themselves from birds and large

↑ Family Ranidae. Tonkin bug-eyed frog, *Theloderma corticale*, Vietnam.

mammals in the wild with aggressive, gaping charges that can be quite surprising when a captive animal displays the same behavior in a vivarium.

South Africa's Hogsback region is home to the Hogsback frog, *Anhydrophryne rattrayi*. Male Hogsback frogs dig chambers with their noses in moist soil. Females lay eggs, which develop directly into froglets.

The Goliath frog, *Conraua goliath*, is the world's largest frog; it grows to about 13 inches long (33 cm) and can weigh up to 6 pounds (2.7 kg). Goliaths live in fast-flowing rivers in rainforests in western Africa.

Male Goliath frogs do not call because they have no vocal sac. Mating is a collision of the titans as the males grasp and clasp the females while they lay eggs. Adult Goliath frogs eat just about anything, but their tadpoles eat only certain waterfall-restricted water plants.

← Family Ranidae. Pig frog, *Rana grylio*, South-eastern U.S., introduced in China, the Bahamas and Puerto Rico.

Otherwise the tadpoles are quite ordinary in appearance and size. However, once the tadpoles transform, they grow to enormous size.

Stretched out, adult Goliath frogs can measure, nose to toe, a foot or two (30–60 cm). Holding one is described as holding a plastic bag of soggy sand. As recently as the late 1960s, Goliath frogs had only to worry about being eaten for food. Now, deforestation in western Africa of about 200,000 acres (81,000 ha) annually for lumber products and conversion to agriculture threatens their habitat. Agrochemicals and chemicals used in illegal fishing are also polluting their rivers.

The Government of Cameroon established three wildlife sanctuaries, but dam construction and the international wildlife trade still threaten the largest frog in the world. They are still unprotected by international treaty. Local people collect the frogs, which can bring $5 U.S. at market. They are associated with purity because of where they live and are considered a good food for pregnant women. Goliath frogs were exported to zoos, but breeding programs have been unsuccessful and they don't survive well in captivity.

Asia

Ranids are spread over the continent. The Indian green frog, *Rana hexadactyla,* is the only known leaf-eating frog. Plant material accounts for nearly 80 percent of its food.

In Sri Lanka, male *Nyctimantis spp.* watch over their eggs, which are deposited on leaves that hang over streams. When the eggs hatch, the tadpoles fall into the water below and finish developing into frogs.

In Borneo, male *Rana finchi* watch over egg clutches laid on land and transport the tadpoles to water on their backs.

The legs of Asian bullfrogs, *Hoplobatrachus tigerinus,* are harvested in the millions for food each year.

Europe

The edible frog, *Rana esculenta,* and the European common frog, *Rana temporaria,* have been known since ancient times and are shown in Roman mosaics and other ancient art. The edible frog is reportedly a hybrid of the marsh and pond frogs of Europe. The European common frog is found north of the Arctic Circle and is often described as the northernmost frog on Earth.

↓ Family Ranidae. A male edible frog, *Rana esculenta*, has both vocal sacs inflated. Europe.

↑ Family Ranidae. Wood frog, *Rana sylvatica*, northern North America.

↓ Family Ranidae. Two American bullfrogs, *Rana catesbeiana*, photographed in Pennsylvania. The species has been introduced worldwide for food.

North America

Tadpoles of the American bullfrog, *Rana catesbeiana*, spend a year in water before transforming into froglets, which spend most of their time in or near permanent water. Bullfrogs were exported to Europe for food. Some escaped and have, as bullfrogs do, eaten their way through the local fauna – including other frogs. Tabloids have had headlines like "Invasion of the Killer Frogs." Naturalized bullfrogs are also reported that originated in Asia, where they were bred for food and some were released by well-meaning individuals. They eat anything they can catch and cram into their mouths – birds, snakes, mammals, other frogs and fish.

The quiet wood frog, *Rana sylvatica*, lives from temperate North America to the treeline in the Arctic. Its soft call is similar to a duck's quacking, but you have to be within about 30 feet (9 m) to hear it. The call changes when the male encounters a female, and then it stops. They are one of the earliest spring breeders. Wood frogs lay their eggs communally in relatively shallow spring ponds. The dark embryos absorb heat, which is conserved by the jelly-like protective layers. This practice can raise the temperature of the pond by about 10°F (6°C).

Other North American Ranids include the painfully shy pig frog, *Rana grylio,* which wasn't discovered until years after its noisy relative, the bullfrog. The females can lay 10,000 eggs, which form a surface film on the water and can stick to emergent vegetation. Depending on temperature, the tadpoles mature in one season or overwinter and transform the following year.

Family *Rhacophoridae*
Afro-Asian Treefrogs

The nearly 300 species of Afro-Asian treefrogs are separated into 14 genera, from sub-Saharan Africa, Madagascar, India, Sri Lanka, southeast Asia and Indonesia to the southern islands of Japan.

Some Rhacophorids have direct development, but most whip up foam nests attached to leaves and other vegetation in trees overhanging water. When the eggs hatch, the tadpoles drop out and into the water.

The famous flying frogs of Malaysia, Reinwardt's flying frog, *Rhacophorus reinwardtii* and Wallace's flying frog, *Rhacophorus nigropalmatus,* have huge webbing between their fingers and toes which they use to slow their fall out of trees and glide. Although nicknamed "flying frogs," a more accurate description would be "not quite falling frogs."

↓ **Reinwardt's flying frog, *Rhacophorus reinwardtii.***

↑ Family Rhacophoridae. Bright-eyed frogs, *Boophis idae*, Madagascar.

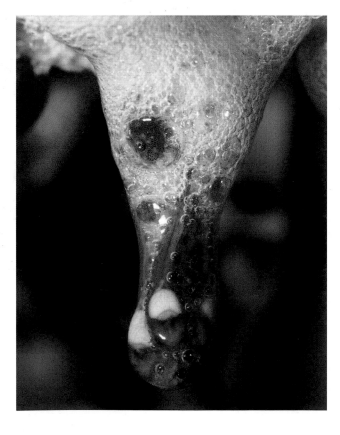

The Malaysian hill froglet, *Philautus vermiculatus,* is a bubble-nest frog. Reportedly, several males gather around and help froth up the nest, competing to fertilize the eggs as the female lays them.

Foam-nesting treefrogs, including African gray treefrogs, *Chiromantis xerampelina,* have their front four fingers arranged in a unique way. Two digits oppose the other two, permitting *Chiromantis spp.* to grip twigs very tightly. These treefrogs also can spend great periods of time out of water as they are very resistant to drying out.

← Family Rhacophoridae. Egg mass of the foam-nest treefrog, *Chiromantis xerampelina,* eastern and southern Africa.

Family *Mantellidae*
Mantellas

Mantella frogs are brightly colored and have toxic skin secretions. In both of these ways, they resemble, but are not related to, South American poison frogs, although some authors have classified them with Dendrobatids as well as with the Old World treefrogs.

Mantellas occur only on Madagascar and, like many of the other animals and plants native to that fertile island, some have been pushed to the brink of extinction by human activities including deforestation and international commerce. About 25,000 frogs a year were being exported until local and international laws protected them in the 1990s. The John G. Shedd Aquarium in Chicago has bred six different species of mantellas, gaining important knowledge that may be useful for conserving the species.

Mantellas are tiny; most are between one-half and one inch long (12.5–25 mm). They are often described as living jewels; their bright body colors include green, blue, red, orange or yellow, usually on a black background.

Most mantellas live boldly on land, in moist places including decaying logs. Adult mantellas hunt and eat termites, ants and other small insects in daylight. Males defend their territory, which may include a broken, water-filled bamboo stalk. Two of the 14 known species deposit eggs in water; the rest lay them in damp and humid terrestrial locations. Water-breeding mantellas often provide extra eggs for tadpole nourishment, and elaborate parenting behavior has been described for several of the species. All mantellas are photogenic.

↑ Family Mantellidae. Golden mantella, *Mantella aurantiaca,* is one of the smallest of this family.

↓ Family Mantellidae. Painted mantella, *Mantella madagascariensis,* eastern Madagascar.

3 Anatomy & Physiology

CHAPTER THREE

Anatomy & Physiology

WHAT MAKES A FROG a frog and not a fish or a dog? Early on, people recognized both frogs and toads as distinct types of organisms. Frogs were familiar and well known to everyone because they lived in just about every damp, moist or wet spot on Earth – and quite a few dry ones as well. Our ancestors saw frogs around their homes and farms when they drew water or washed clothes, as well as when they traveled on or crossed rivers, ponds and streams.

Frogs were kept as folk-barometers and for food. Frog legs have long been on the menu. Recipes for them can be found in books all the way back to the Roman Empire.

The availability of frogs, and their similarity in appearance to very tiny people, led to their early and continuing use as a research substitute for humans. In the first recorded frog experiment in 1487, Leonardo da Vinci (1452–1519) discovered that a frog's brain controls all its other organs.

In an effort to confirm or deny folk-tales and legends, other early anatomists and naturalists searched for the mythical toadstone, which was supposed to be the cure for various diseases. After experimentation, which involved many sleepless nights watching toads and expecting to see them produce the stones, geologist and royal physician Anselm Boetius de Boodt (1550–1632) wrote in 1609: "*Ab eo tempore pro nugis habui quod de Bufonio lapide, ejusque origine traditur.*" ("From that time on I regarded as nonsense what has been handed down touching the toad-stone and its origin.")

In the new spirit of experimentation, Thomas Browne (1605–82) studied living frogs. In 1672, he described frog reproduction from spawning to adult-

← Golden toads, *Bufo periglenes,* in the mating clasp called "amplexus." Note the pattern difference between the golden male on top and the particolored female below. These beautiful toads haven't been seen since the late 1980s and are feared extinct.

←← Indian bullfrogs, *Hoplobatrachus tigerinus,* used to be called *Rana tigrina.* The name change shows they are now considered less closely related to American bullfrogs, *Rana catesbeiana.*

hood and dispelled the myth of spontaneous generation from pond slime. He also dispensed another bit of common folklore when he discovered that frogs will not drown, but instead may die if kept away from water. Anton van Leeuwenhoek (1632–1723) began dissecting under his microscopes and studied frog organ systems, tadpoles and eggs. Accidental discoveries by Luigi Galvani (1737–98) revealed that the nerves transmit information by electrical impulses.

In the mid-18th century, Carl von Linné (1707–78) defined the plant and animal kingdoms according to anatomical characters, but it wasn't until 1804 that amphibians were placed in their own order, separate from fish and reptiles. Even today, many biology books cover frogs and toads in a few paragraphs and a "life-cycle of the frog" diagram, and continue as if the more than 4,000 living species with their amazing and successful adaptations had nothing more to tell us about life's incredible journey through time.

Frogs and toads are amphibians. Like their relatives, the salamanders and caecilians, they are said to "lead a double life," which refers to their most common life cycle.

While other vertebrates lay eggs and give live birth, amphibians have the only free-larval phase in any vertebrate group. Adult frogs do not look like or live like their larvae, called tadpoles or pollywogs. Tadpoles have tails, are vegetarian and have forward-facing eyes. Adult frogs do not have tails, are almost all fully carnivorous and have bulging eyes on the tops of their heads. In general, toads tend to have more forward-facing eyes than frogs do, but these features are still different from the tadpole eyes.

For thousands of years, humans have recognized that toads are very frog-like, but not exactly the same. When scientists began to study how frogs and toads are related to each other they found that toads are not a natural group because they are not all descended from one single ancestor. The character-

↓ Cold-tolerant northern cricket frogs, *Acris crepitans*, were once one of the most common amphibians of the upper midwest of both the U.S. and Canada. Now it's rare to see these tiny brightly colored frogs hopping around like the crickets after whom they are named. Curiously, they are still common at the southern end of their range.

From Egg to Frog

1 An egg mass

Frog eggs are often used for scientific and developmental studies because they are transparent. Here, black frog embryos and their diffuse yolk cells are suspended in the egg jelly, equivalent to "egg white," in a developing egg mass.

2 A newly hatched tadpole

Amphibians are the only vertebrates with a free-larval phase. In frogs, individuals in this phase are called tadpoles or pollywogs. Tadpoles are either fully aquatic or develop within their own egg mass. This one is a free-swimming tadpole. Its gills provide oxygen, although most gas respiration occurs across the skin, just as it will in adulthood. Tadpoles are either filter feeders or algae eaters; most are vegetarian and have the long gut required to digest vegetable matter. A tadpole has to eat a lot to become an adult frog.

3 Early metamorphosis

When the hind legs begin to form, the tadpole is entering the metamorphosis phase, during which it will transform to an adult frog. About now, it is losing its gills and growing lungs. It starts to surface frequently, gulping precious air and trying not to be eaten at the same time.

4 Middle metamorphosis

When the front legs are developing, tadpoles begin to fast – eating nothing until metamorphosis is complete – for two reasons. First, their tadpole mouth parts re-form into an adult jaw and tongue; second, their long, vegetarian digestive system needs to stay empty to re-form to a short, carnivorous gut. Hormones moderate these and equally dramatic transformations in other organs as the tadpole continues its amazing journey to adulthood.

5 A young froglet

Metamorphosis ends at slightly different times of development for different species. This young froglet has left the water, even though its tail is not completely gone. Soon it will be a fully developed adult.

↑ The translucent skin of La Palma glass frogs, *Hyalinobatrachium valerioi*, reveals arteries, veins and pigment cells.

which they spread and glide.

Treefrogs have enlarged tips, called toepads, on the ends of all their digits. These help them stick to trees and leaves. In the breeding season, males of some species develop calluses, called claspers or nuptial pads, on their inner fingers. These help the males hold onto their slippery mates during spawning and may be darker than the rest of the forehand.

Frogs and toads that do a lot of digging tend to have keratinized spades on their hind legs. Keratin is a hard material that protects the softer skin within from the abrasion of sand and other sharp materials in the soil.

Internal Organs

Like all vertebrates, a frog's heart pumps blood through arteries, into capillaries and back to the heart by way of veins. The blood carries nutrients, gases, hormones and other vital cells. Additionally frogs have a well-developed lymph system different than most other vertebrates.

Tadpoles breathe with internal gills, while adult frogs usually have lungs. Both tadpoles and adults are also capable of transferring gases across their highly permeable skins.

Feeding

Amphibians have a relatively unspecialized digestive system. Anything that will fit goes into the mouth, down the short esophagus and into the stomach. Unless some part or piece falls off the prey item, it is eaten whole.

Frogs can either stuff food in their mouths with their forelimbs or use their amazing tongues. Frog tongues are attached at the front of the mouth. When the prey is in range, the tongue flicks out to catch and draw prey into the mouth.

Studies have shown that toads are more efficient tongue hunters than frogs, hitting a target dead on nearly every single time. In some species, about 2 inches (5 cm) of tongue comes flying out at the prey. Studies have shown that sticky secretions glue the tongue onto the food item. Pipid frogs have no tongues. They just slurp in food from the water using their fingers to help push. Many other frogs will assist the tongue by pushing with their forelimbs.

Frogs have efficient digestive enzymes to help break down the fur, bones and hard parts that they consume along with the more nutritious bits. Frogs have large livers because they store a starch called glycogen, which they use to survive long periods without meals. Some species in the northern latitudes can go six months or more over the winter without eating. They emerge powered up and ready to breed in the spring.

Frogs release urine that is less salty than their blood. Frogs have to maintain their osmotic balance with the environment. Their urine is mostly water; they discharge as much as 33 percent of their body weight per day. In dry areas, however, frogs and toads conserve and recycle moisture and do not need to excrete such large amounts of liquid. Frogs also get rid of waste liquid through their skin.

Senses and Communication

Frogs are wary and careful because they are on the menu for many other creatures. Thus they have evolved extraordinary sensory and communication systems, including familiar visual and auditory systems as well as less common ones, including the lateral-line organ and statoacoustic organ system.

Eyes

Frog eyes serve their owners well. A frog's spherical eyes are protected by eyelids and lubricated by moisture-producing glands. The eyes are also protected by a "third eyelid," called the nictitating membrane. A frog focuses its eyes by moving the lens back and forth – the action is like sharpening the image in a spyglass or telephoto lens. Frogs hunt by sight and can see close things well, but the background is out of focus. They are exceptionally good at seeing movement against the fuzzy background.

Frogs' eyes either blend into their overall pattern or punctuate it. Both iris color and pupil shape vary from species to species. The pupil controls the amount of light reaching the retina, and its shape is considered key to image formation and interpretation.

↓ This red-eyed treefrog, *Agalychnis callidryas*, has narrowed its pupils in response to the photographer's powerful studio lights.

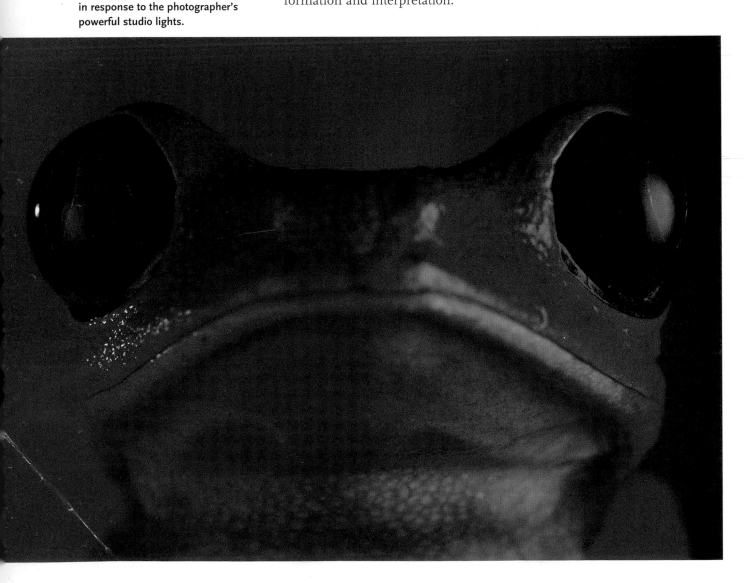

FROGS

Most North American frogs have horizontal pupils as do many species on the other continents, including the green and golden bell frog, *Litoria aurea*, which was the mascot of the 2000 Sydney Olympics in Australia. The widely distributed marine or cane toad, *Bufo marinus*, has a horizontal pupil within a golden iris. White's treefrog, *Litoria caerulea*, has a horizontal pupil in a speckled and iridescent eye.

Central and South American treefrogs and a few North American frogs have vertical pupils as do other species around the world, including the Australian Mallee spadefoot toad, *Neobatrachus pictus*, and the giant burrowing frog, *Heleioporus australiacus*. The supermodels of the frog family, red-eyed treefrogs, *Agalychnis callidryas*, have vertical pupils that become round in low light. They live in Central America, but are widely held in captivity. This frog is so widely shown in photos, on the covers of frog books and pamphlets, that it has become a global icon for frogs in general.

Tomato frogs, *Dyscophus antongilii*, have round pupils. Fire-bellied toads, *Bombina spp.*, have triangular to nearly heart-shaped pupils. In Australia, Peron's treefrog, *Litoria peronii*, has cross-shaped pupils and is also known as the maniacal cackle frog to the people who have to live around its breeding ponds. Other frog pupils are diamond shaped and some even look like hourglasses. Look at the eyes in photographs of frogs and toads and you can see whether it was taken with a flash, with a mounted light, or outside in natural light.

As beautiful as they are, a frog's eyes have a job to do. Studies have shown that frogs confused by two visual stimuli will often freeze up and not react. If there is only one clear and present danger, the frog will leap away.

A breathtaking study of frog and toad visual abilities looked at how frequently the tongue actually hit a televised image of a cricket. The researcher found that toads hit the target more often than frogs did. Additionally, when the program ended, the frogs just sat still. The toads, however, looked behind the television as if to see if the crickets were lurking back there.

Movies of frog and toad locomotion show that when toads walk fast, they close their eyes during part of each step. Frogs and toads may have developed this characteristic to keep them from becoming dizzy from the amount of visual stimulus reaching the brain.

Muscles behind frog and toad eyes help push food down the throat. The forceful eye-blinking is often accompanied by a rapid opening and closing of the mouth and waving of the hands.

Frog Calling

Male frogs make loud calls to attract females in the breeding season. They keep their mouths closed, breathe in through the nose, and pass the air back and forth from lungs to mouth. They also may pressurize their own ears, so they don't hear their own call full strength.

Male frogs may use one or two vocal sacs to call. Some species without a vocal sac still manage to call. Perhaps they are using their tympana to amplify their vocalizations. Other frogs use natural echoes, and sometimes caves, culverts and tunnels, to amplify the sounds made by their larynx and vocal cords.

North American gray treefrogs, *Hyla versicolor* and *Hyla chrysoscelis,* have one vocal sac, while *Rana pipiens, Rana sphenocephala, Rana areolata* and *Rana grylio* have two vocal sacs. Male Darwin's frogs, *Rhinoderma darwinii,* nurture their young in their vocal sacs.

Frogs can hear other sounds besides frog calls, and they will respond to noises including music and whistles. Research in the early 20th century showed that frogs cannot learn to associate sounds with anything but other frog calls. However, they regularly respond to pressure and humidity changes leading up to rainstorms. This observation resulted in folkloric descriptions of frogs making the rain fall by calling. Some cultures even play music, hoping to make the frogs call down the rains.

Each species of frog, and to a certain degree each population of each species of frog, has its distinct call. Research has shown that males become territorial if calls from farther away are played to them. One student floated speakers on Styrofoam blocks in a midwestern pond, played recordings of distant males, and then sat back in amazement when the frogs swam out and attacked his speakers.

Some frog calls are very quiet and can be heard only a short distance from the frog, but some frog calls are extremely loud. Calls of the Puerto Rican coqui frog, *Eleutherodactylus coqui,* have been measured at between 90 and 95 decibels at a half-meter distance (about 20 inches). At the same distance, a jackhammer registers 100 decibels. The first part of their call, "co," has been found to be territorial and is noticed by other males; the second part, "qui," gets a reaction from the females.

Not surprisingly, the more frog calls researched, the greater the variety of calls discerned. One of the most obvious ways to sex male and female frogs during the breeding season is also one of the easiest. Male frogs clasped gently under their forelegs let out a little chirp known as a "release call."

Females do not react to the clasping, and remain silent. In nature, the release call notifies the clasping male that he has another male in his clutches.

Warning, or alarm, calls are given by some frogs as they leap into streams or ponds when predators or people approach. This is the only frog call known to be made when the frog has its mouth open. Another kind of call is a territorial call between two male frogs. Ignoring a territorial call may end up in a frog wrestling match as the owner of the territory takes on the intruder. Some frogs have a rain call, which is most likely the source of all the folktales of how frogs foretell storms.

Frogs do not just call during the actual mating period. Some warm up for a few weeks before hibernation, and emerge ready to sing their hearts out in the spring. Others anticipate the mating period and call a little each day in advance, especially during high humidity or showers. Female frogs in some species also make noises that, sometimes, approach the male call. Both males and females also make noises with other parts of their bodies. Sometimes they vibrate their tympana at the surface of the water to make a clicking noise. Certain frogs will swat the surface of the water or the ground.

Researchers use frog calls to study frog populations, and they study the calls themselves. Writers have tried to describe the sounds of frogs; some are like banjos, others are like pebbles clicking, and still others are like rooms full of chuckling old men. With the advent of lightweight, relatively water-proof technology in the 1950s, Chuck Bogert (1908–92), a researcher from the American Museum of Natural History in New York, began to record the sounds made by frogs and toads. His landmark recordings taught North

→ Never judge a frog by its skinsuit. Dull American toads, *Bufo americanus*, conceal a vivid surprise – a bright blue vocal sac, which they use to produce an unexpectedly sweet trill.

How a Frog Hears

- Each frog's eardrum, called the tympanum, is formed by a membrane tightly stretched on a ring of cartilage. The eardrum vibrates

- A rod connected to the eardrum pushes the inner ear fluid back and forth.

- The fluid causes hairs in hair cells to wave.

- The hair cells touch nerve fibers.

- The nerves carry electrical impulses to the brain, where the signal is interpreted.

American frog calls to generations of herpetologists. As the technology continues to improve, other people have recorded local populations, digitized the recordings and posted them on the world wide web. Learning frog calls is easier with recorded media. Remember, however, that each pond has its own dialect and some frog calls may sound quite different from the way they sound on the recording. Some species call differently at different temperatures. Studying frog calls with a local biologist or naturalist is often the best way to learn the sounds made by the local frog fauna.

The major disadvantage for frogs making all this noise is that many predators can hear, too. Besides the usual birds, small mammals and fish, perhaps the most curious frog predator that locates frogs by their sound is the frog-eating fringe-lipped bat, *Trachops cirrhosus,* of Central America.

Hearing

The frog's hearing system is used primarily to hear sounds made by other frogs and predators at close range. Besides their eardrums, frogs have another way to hear sound. A direct air link between their eardrums and their lungs permits the frogs to locate the source of a sound and may be used to protect their own ears from loud frog choruses. This connection can be used to equalize pressure between the lungs and the two surfaces of their eardrums. While it hasn't been proven, it is possible this connection also alerts the frogs to changes in barometric pressure in much the same way that human ears "pop" in an airplane or a fast elevator.

When some frogs can't hear well because of the noise of fast-flowing streams, they use forearm signaling instead of calling.

← Food or not food, that is the question. Toads, like this woodhouse's toad, *Bufo woodhousii*, are successful visual hunters. One tongue-flick and the item is headed into the stomach, where it joins as many as a thousand others each day.

Other Sensory Organs

Frogs have other sensory systems. In addition to eyes, ears and touch, they have chemical senses, plus a lateral-line and statoacoustic organ system.

Frogs can taste with their tongue and can sense salty, bitter, sweet and sour. Their sense of smell is important; they use it to recognize good places to spawn as well as to find potential mates.

Most swimming tadpoles, as well as adult discoglossid and clawed frogs, have an interesting sense organ known as the lateral-line organ. It detects movement of the water, whether within the water column or at the surface, and is a characteristic shared with fish and some other amphibians. Fire-bellied toads, *Bombina spp.,* use their lateral-line organ during breeding. Other species probably use it for things researchers haven't yet imagined.

The statoacoustic organ system does several things for frogs. It helps them balance and contributes information to their sense of hearing. The organ is composed of a labyrinthine folding of tissue, filled with lymphatic fluid. The various parts of this organ help the frog stay level in water, turn 360 degrees at any time and still maintain spatial control and detect substrate vibrations.

↑ The young American bullfrog, *Rana catesbeiana*, on the left is older than the one on the right, which still has its long tadpole tail.

Skin and Parotoid Glands

Frogs have permeable skin, which means they can transfer water and gases through their skin. Different species use this ability in different ways, but some frogs can get more than half their air without using their lungs. In addition, they may have particularly thin skin on the part of the hindquarters that sits right on the ground. They can soak up moisture from the ground just by sitting on it. Inside the skin are specialized cells that pump salt into the frog to keep the animal in osmotic balance with water. These are used by most species in breeding season, and full time by aquatic frogs.

All frogs shed regularly in a process called exuviation. Frog sheds are rarely seen, however, because frogs eat their sheds to prevent the loss of salts and nutrients from the skin.

When they were ready, my captive frogs and toads worked off their skin. They then passed it over the head and into the mouth with such a smooth move that I never managed to get even so much as a piece of skin. They started working off their skin by rubbing and scraping against rough surfaces. The skin peeled off rapidly from back to front once the frog or toad got started. After the head piece popped, the animal looked a little disoriented for a split second, then stuffed the skin into its mouth using its forelimbs, closed its mouth and pushed down with its eyes. A quick blink and the skin was gone.

Frog skin can also provide excellent camouflage. Some frogs look like leaves in the undergrowth. Others sport bright colors, which can be seen clearly against the natural background.

The outermost layer of the skin is the epidermis, which is composed

mostly of keratinized cells. Keratin is a tough, waterproof protein. This layer is pierced by the openings of glands that release various fluids. Some fluids moisturize the frog, others help the frog pass various gases, and still others are toxic or defensive.

Special shape-changing cells in frog skin, called chromatophores, hold the pigments that give frogs their palette. The chromatophores expand and contract, revealing or hiding the pigment concealed within.

The names of chromatophores are based on the pigment color or iridescent platelet cells they contain.

Under a low-power microscope or a hand lens, the top layer of frog skin, the epidermis, looks transparent, translucent or white. In many species, the next layer down has chromatophores full of black pigment. As the frogs change temperature, or are stressed, their black-holding chromatophores stretch and thin and the frog changes shading – becoming lighter. When the chromatophores expand again, the skin appears darker. Cold frogs are usually darker than warm frogs. Dry toads appear lighter in color than they do after a good soaking. Frogs bustling about become lighter in color, too. Perhaps their own increased metamorphic activity causes the chromatophores to retract.

Additionally, since every chromatophore is connected to the nervous system under the control of the frog's brain, the frog can change color when it wants to, regardless of external conditions.

If frogs have no accessory pigments, their colors will be dull grays and browns. Yellow colors are a result of yellow pigments, but the common "frog greens" are actually a result of a special interference layer and two pigments, black and yellow. If the polygonal cells in the interference layer contain

↑ Frog coloration can be brilliant, dull or cryptic: Here more Peruvian toads, *Bufo typhonius complex*, lurk amidst the leaves than are obvious at first glance.

↓ The names of chromatophores are based on the pigment color or iridescent platelet cells they contain.

Pigment	Chromatophore name
Black and brown	melanophores
yellow	xanthophores
red or orange	erythrophores
platelets	iridophores

yellow, the frog looks green. If the cells are empty, the black underpigment shows through a clear or translucent epidermis, producing various shades of blue.

Even the greenest of frogs can have blue or yellow streaks caused by the contraction or expansion of the polygonal cells. A piece of cut-off frog skin seen from below is always black because the color is all on the top surface. Some species, including the poison frogs, have metallic, red, white and iridescent pigments in their polygonal cells. Coupled with the colors contained in their chromatophores, these give them the brilliant appearance of living jewels.

Some frogs have brightly colored bellies, which they reveal if startled. This "unken reflex" is also seen in other vertebrates. In every case it is a warning. It means, "Eat at your own risk."

Mutations sometimes give rise to albino frogs, which look yellow, cream or white and have no black pigment anywhere on their bodies, including their eyes. An albino frog doesn't last long in the wild. It has trouble seeing, is easy to spot and so becomes an easy morsel for a hungry predator.

Toxins and Secretions

Toxic is relative. Compounds secreted by the African clawed frog, *Xenopus laevis,* called magainins are deadly to bacteria, causing cytolysis, the rupture of cell walls. This is, however, a positive thing for people because magainins are being tested for their possible beneficial effects in humans.

A drug that reportedly blocks pain two hundred times more effectively than morphine was originally synthesized in 1976 from the skins of Ecuadorian poison frogs, *Epidobates tricolor.* Unfortunately it was too toxic to use in humans, but its structure led researchers to a new human painkiller.

Toad toxicity has been recognized for a long time. German violinists in the 19th century rubbed their hands on toads to reduce perspiration. Meanwhile, researchers were injecting toad toxins through the new hypodermic needle into vertebrate animals and found that toad toxins were invariably fatal if the dose was high enough.

Giant marine or cane toads, *Bufo marinus,* produce a substance called "bufotoxin," which is stored in and released through their parotoid glands. Their toxin is a component of traditional medicine in some parts of Asia, although the species is not native to that continent. There are reports from the early 1990s that bufotoxin was being traded for medical use at about $100 per gram.

Toads' toxicity gives rise to a most dangerous urban legend, that eating toad skin or licking toads will get you high. In reality, licking a toad can get you sick or dead, depending on your general health and body weight. A traditional Chinese medical concoction called Chan Su is made from dried toad skins and contains naturally occurring cardiac steroids. It has a street reputation as an aphrodisiac intended for topical application, but in the early 1990s four people reportedly died from eating it. At about the same time, it was widely reported that several people died in Australia attempting to get high by licking or smoking toad secretions. Since then, fairly aggressive public health campaigns have convinced many Australians that cane toads are "deadly toxic," as I was told by the daughter of my hostess in Brisbane when I went out to take a photo of the cane toad we caught in their fountain.

American toads, *Bufo americanus,* are eaten by hognose snakes. The

↑ The marine or cane toad, *Bufo marinus*, is considered the most poisonous toad on Earth.

hognose not only has long fangs to puncture and deflate the toad if it puffs up for defense, but is also seemingly immune to the toad's toxins. North American skunks will eat toads, but they may roll them around a bit first. Researchers speculate the skunks do this so that the toad will squirt all its toxin on the ground. Florida's gopher frog eats toads, but spits out the toxin in a foamy white mass.

The poison frogs of South America produce batrachotoxin, one of the most powerful neurotoxins in the world. Native peoples used to roast the frogs slowly to get them to release the toxin, with which they coated their arrow tips or blowgun-dart tips to hunt prey. Early researchers reported that full-grown monkeys would fall dead instantly after being hit by a frog-poisoned dart. Poison frogs, which manufacture this toxin from materials in their natural habitat, are not toxic in captivity.

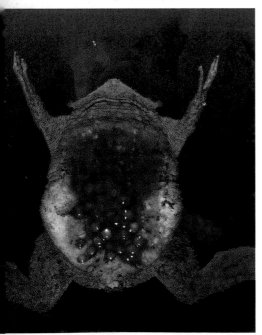

↑ A smaller male Map treefrog, *Hyla geographica*, clasps the larger and brighter female on a leaf in South America.

↓ A female Surinam toad, *Pipa pipa*, with eggs on its back, where they will stay until they hatch.

Physiology

A LARGE NUMBER of physiology experiments have been performed on frogs over the years. Many are repeated year after year in high school and college biology laboratories. Of these experiments, few teach much about what it means to be a live amphibian. Instead, they tell us a lot about the narrowness of human research and education.

Most biology books reiterate that amphibians are cold-blooded, or ectothermic, animals and state that frogs and toads are totally dependent on exterior temperatures to regulate their internal temperature. This has been proven false by researchers who found that frogs do control their body temperature, although not to the degree that mammals can.

Frogs seek sun or shade to assist in maintaining optimal temperature conditions. Some become nocturnal in the heat of the summer. Others cool off by finding a damp spot or wet pond.

Frogs can survive long periods of total inactivity during adverse conditions. In cold places, they hibernate underground or in mud or sand. In hot, dry places, frogs estivate in the ground, in cracks in rocks, in wet spots in talus slopes, and in and around the roots of plants. But frogs have to react to outside conditions, too. North American wood frogs, *Rana sylvatica,* can freeze about a third of their bodies and stay alive with a body temperature of about 21°F (–6°C) for about a week. When the temperatures rise again, they thaw ready to breed.

Frog Food

Frogs eat a lot when active and not at all when they are inactive. Frogs hunt in an area from their left knee to their right knee and extended out about two body lengths. At the longer distances, they may hop and then thrust out their tongues; closer prey can be nabbed by the tongue alone.

Frogs eat just about anything they can catch and shove into their mouths. They eat small mammals, birds, snakes, fish, worms, insects and other invertebrates. Frogs can be active predators or sit-and-wait predators. In some species, the same frog can use both feeding strategies at different times; other species use only one or the other scheme.

Reproduction

Unlike salamanders, which can hold back on transformation and breed while still in the larval phase, frogs breed only after metamorphosis to their adult form.

Breeding is biologically expensive – especially for the female, who provides not only half the genetic material but also all the nourishment for the egg phase. In species that overwinter or oversummer before breeding season, all that energy is stored inside the frog before it begins to hibernate or estivate. Frogs emerge from dormancy in breeding condition and raring to go. Males usually appear at the ponds first. Their calling is a guide to the females.

Male frogs tend to be smaller than the females because eggs take more energy to produce and more space to store than is required to make and store much smaller sperm cells. Eggs are formed in the female's ovaries and are haploid; they have one-half the number of chromosomes that will be found in the adult animal. Male frogs produce and release haploid sperm; when one fuses with an egg, the two halves of the genetic material form the template for the adult animal.

Males make distinctive mating calls, but they stop calling quickly when they find a female. In the mating embrace, called amplexus, male frogs clasp the females like little backpacks. They hold on, sometimes for a day or even longer. In all but tailed frogs, the female releases eggs while the male releases sperm, which fertilizes the eggs. To prove the rule that there is an exception for everything in nature, tailed frogs, *Ascaphus truei*, have a copulatory organ and internal fertilization.

Once the eggs are fertilized, some species lay on land, some attached to vegetation, and some in frothy foam nests. Others lay huge egg masses directly in water. Eggs can be laid singly or in large clutches, with great care or none at all. A female marine or cane toad, *Bufo marinus*, can lay up to 35,000 eggs in long strands that look like dark dots in clear jelly. Some of the world's tiniest frogs lay only one egg.

Unlike the eggs of higher vertebrates, which have an amnion, frog eggs do not have embryonic membranes. Lacking an amnion to protect the developing embryo restricts frog eggs to moist or wet places. Frog eggs do not have a well-defined yolk sac. Instead, the yolk is stored in individual cells diffused throughout the egg.

After fertilization, the cells in the egg divide, grow and divide over and over again until the tadpole is formed. In some American toads, such as *Bufo americanus* and *Bufo woodhousii*, this can be as little as two days. Other frogs lay eggs that take weeks and months to develop.

Most frogs are oviparous: the eggs are laid and hatch outside the mother's body. Only animals that nourish their unborn young by means of an umbil-

↑ American bullfrog, *Rana catesbeiana*, eating a very large worm.

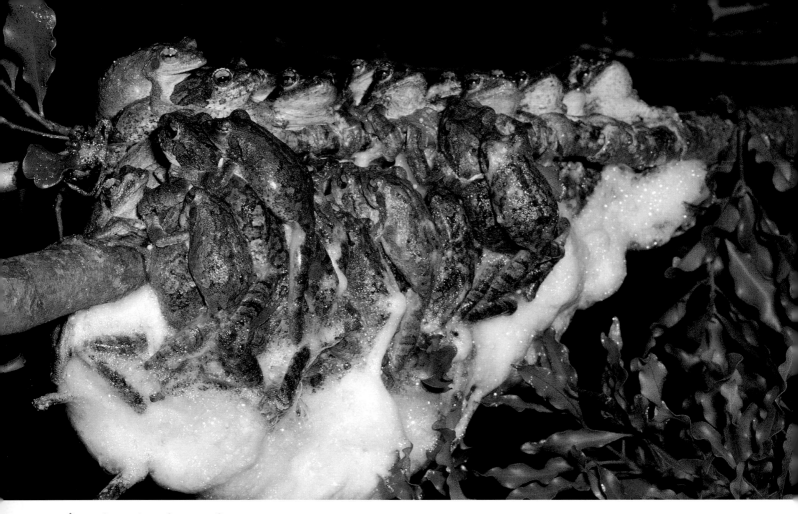

↑ Nearly two dozen foam nest frogs, *Chiromantis xerampelina*, show how they got their name kicking up a frothy home for their fresh laid eggs.

ical cord and placenta are called viviparous. Since no frog has this anatomy, the so-called viviparous toad of Africa is misnamed and should just be called a live-bearing toad. It and the few other frogs that give birth to live young are actually ovoviviparous. Their eggs develop directly, skipping the tadpole phase, and form a froglet inside the mother's body from which it emerges as a tiny adult.

Other frogs have direct development from egg to froglet, but this doesn't take place inside their own bodies. The eggs are laid in moist places; they develop into froglets without leaving the protective membrane. Most frogs, however, have indirect development. This means that the egg grows and forms the tadpole, which later becomes a froglet. Most tadpoles are free-swimming after hatching, but some live in nests until they emerge as adult frogs. The amount of time needed for this process is highly variable.

There are two kinds of tadpoles: filter feeders and algae eaters. Filter-feeding tadpoles are mostly tropical – members of the families Pipidae, Rhinophrynidae and Microhylidae. There is some evidence that the only extinct frog family, Paleobatrachidae, may have had filter-feeding tadpoles.

All tadpoles have gills, which move oxygen from the water into their blood-stream. Molecule for molecule, however, most gas respiration occurs across their skin and into the bloodstream, just as it does in the adults. Some tadpoles use their gills to filter feed, but not as the primary feeding apparatus.

Algae-eating tadpoles are wide-bodied with broad tails and a floppy mouth-part called an oral disk. In the middle of the disk are rows and rows of tiny keratin teeth as well as a beak. The tadpole opens its mouth an amazing

← Eggs stream from two spawning pair of golden toads, *Bufo periglenes.* Notice how differently colored are the females below the bright yellow males.

↓ The eyes of these plains spadefoot toads, *Spea bombifrons,* show they are in the process of metamorphosis to adulthood as their shallow puddle dries around them.

→ Two La Palma glass frogs,
Hyalinobatrachium valerioi,
guarding their egg masses.

Nest Piracy

Recently researchers have found an unusual mating strategy, called "nest piracy," employed by some male European common frogs, *Rana temporaria.* As in many frogs, males and females pair off and clasp, then females release eggs and males release a cloud of sperm that fertilizes most of the eggs in the cluster. What is newly known is that males that didn't succeed in finding a female to clasp may follow a breeding pair and wait until they're done and leave the egg cluster. Then the pirate male digs into the cluster and refertilizes the entire mass. The unfertilized eggs are now fertilized – by the second male. The process benefits both the female, whose effort to produce the eggs is not wasted, and also the nonpaired male, who might otherwise not be able to reproduce in that season.

180 degrees and lays it flat on the surface to be scraped clean of algae. The teeth then grasp the surface while the beak slashes off the algae. The teeth then clean off any missed vegetation, and the tadpole moves on. The action has been compared with the typical double-bladed razor; one blade cuts, and the other finishes the trim. The process is extremely fast, since the tadpole needs to eat a lot to become an adult frog.

Various difficult environmental conditions may turn ordinary vegetarian tadpoles into cannibals that consume the other tadpoles in the pond or aquarium. Spadefoot toads are particularly noted for cannibalistic larva.

Metamorphosing tadpoles begin to grow back legs, lose their gills and grow lungs. Then they have to gulp air from the surface of the water and not get eaten by predators. At about the same time as their front legs begin to develop, tadpoles stop eating because their long and winding vegetarian digestive system is being re-formed into a shorter carnivorous gut. Tadpole eyes metamorphose, too. Adult frogs can see both in and out of water.

The tadpole's specialized keratin mouthparts re-form into the adult jaw, and it grows a tongue. The inner ear replaces the lateral-line organ, and many other dramatic and fundamental anatomical changes occur during metamorphosis. Researchers have found that hormones are highly important during the metamorphic process. The end of metamorphosis is considered to be the time the tadpole leaves the water or terrestrial nest and begins its free-living adult phase as a tiny frog. It may still have a tail for a short while, but it is a fully developed adult animal at the end of a long and difficult transformation.

↑ A Ranid tadpole which has grown its hind legs rests on a submerged branch.

4 Environment & Adaptation

CHAPTER FOUR

Environment & Adaptation

FROGS ARE WONDERFULLY ADAPTED for all types of habitats; they live in places as far south as the bottom of South America and as far north as the Arctic Circle in both the New and Old Worlds.

Some frogs are cosmopolitan generalists that do well in a wide variety of conditions, including those disturbed by humans. Generalists tend to be colonizers. They change habitats following a disturbance, and are likely to travel long distances and become established far from home. As natural habitats become more and more restricted, frog fauna becomes more and more specialized. Superspecialists that occur only in one place are called endemic species. They are most likely to become extinct in accidents, called "stochastic events" by conservation biologists.

Some frogs are fully aquatic, while others are specialized for desert conditions. In general, mountains tend to host a high frog diversity. Like other organisms, frogs can change elevation as the optimal temperatures and moisture conditions move up and down. Globally, the Neotropics of Middle and South America have the highest frog diversity.

At the time frogs evolved, all the continents were joined or joining to form a landmass known as "Pangaea" (see the map on page 21). Northern Pangaea was called "Laurasia," and the conjoined southern continents – now known as South America, Africa, India, Antarctica and Australia – were "Gondwanaland." As the continents rifted apart, frog species were split and carried along with their landscape. Frogs, therefore, were able to colonize the whole Earth without having to cross oceans.

The study of fossil frogs and the biogeography of living families provides some interesting tales of life over time, allowing us to see how the animals moved in response to changing habitats and conditions.

← The Pacific treefrog, *Pseudacris regilla*, is common up and down the Western U.S. and even high in the Sierra Nevada Mountains, where it is almost the only frog left in significant numbers. The others have been lost to trout stocking, chemical drift, disease and habitat modification.

←← An American bullfrog, *Rana catesbeiana*, partially submerged and hidden in duckweed.

↑ Three male common toads, *Bufo bufo*, attempt to mate with a single female.

Frogs appear to have colonized Australia in three waves. The first group of species was in place on Gondwanaland prior to its breakup and has had a long time to disperse widely. When the Australian plate started to rejoin southern Asia about 15 million years ago, a second wave of frogs from Asia arrived on the subcontinent. These frogs are mostly restricted to the Cape York Peninsula of northern Queensland. Finally, the cane toad, *Bufo marinus,* was introduced in 1935 and has spread from north to south along the eastern margin of the continent in just 70 years.

More than a hundred million years ago, toads of the genus *Bufo* appear to have evolved somewhere in the middle of a continental mass that would rift apart to become South America and Africa. From South America, they hopped through North America and from there to the Old World. Scientists studying the timing of land bridges and continental movements use the genetic differences of amphibians and other species to help determine paleogeographic relationships.

One such study worked with several families of Indian frogs, compared them with frogs from Africa and Asia, and discovered that Ranid frogs seem to have evolved in India while it was rifting away from Africa and before it collided with Asia 65 million years ago. From this continental life raft, Ranid frogs dispersed outward until they are today found everywhere except most of Australia and the tip of South America.

Each frog family has a story to tell of where it came from and how it moved over time. As climates and conditions changed, frog species responded. Some became extinct when their specialized habitats were destroyed. Others expanded outward as new opportunities arose. Even so, over the vast span of geological time, life to an individual frog remains the same: hatch, transform, mate and die – hopefully not by being eaten alive.

↑ A canyon treefrog, *Hyla arenicolor,* cryptically blends into a granitic rock.

Protective Strategies

FROGS ARE EATEN by just about anything big enough to catch and swallow them, including birds, reptiles, fish, bats and humans. Frogs do everything they can to keep from being another creature's dinner. Their wonderful leap and their ability to see over their backs to keep a wary eye out for an approaching predator are sometimes augmented by distasteful or poisonous toxins that permit them to relax and not be as concerned about being eaten. Toxic frogs and toads tend to have more front-set eyes because they don't need to be as paranoid about seeing behind themselves.

Other protective strategies include camouflage, defensive behavior, the ability to puff up to present a more formidable foe, warning coloration, warning calls, and the production of too many offspring for any one predator to consume them all at a single sitting.

Humans eat frogs, too. As human populations have grown, so has the demand for fresh and frozen frog legs. Few frogs consumed at table are raised for the purpose because frogs are insectivores and it is very hard to raise thousands of insectivores in captivity. Frog farming works in China and other labor-rich places with low wages; taking frogs from the wild is still perceived as an overhead-free operation with great profits.

From 1973 to 1987, France imported about 111 million pounds of frog legs (50 million kg) of which nearly 2.3 million pounds (1 million kg) came from Bangladesh alone. A conservative estimate of 30 frogs per kilogram produces an astonishing 150 million dead frogs. Little to none of this meat

→ A Malayan horned frog, *Megophrys nasuta,* camouflaged on a leaf in Sabah, Borneo.

is tested for parasites, diseases or toxins before sale as food. Live frogs in Asian grocery stores in the United States are usually infected with bacterial red-leg from the stresses of being collected and housed tightly packed in filthy conditions. If the frogs are bought and released by well-meaning people, the bacteria can be passed into the wild as can any parasites, viruses, fungi or other pathogens from the other side of the world.

Whole areas of Asia have been "defrogged," and the consequences on the local environment are considerable. With fewer frogs to eat bugs, more mosquitoes survive; and more insect-borne diseases like malaria result.

In the United States, scientific and commercial collecting of frogs for high school, college and professional laboratory experiments continues, particularly in economically depressed areas where other resources have been depleted.

↑ "If God had wanted us to be
concerned for the plight of the
toads, he would have made them
cute and furry."
– *Dave Barry, U.S. newspaper humorist*

Environmental Dangers

DURING THE 1970s scientists discovered and studied dozens of species new
to science. Within 15 years, many of these newfound species were gone,
some in huge and disgusting death assemblages. Others disappeared
silently, with no clue to the cause of their passing.

Nobody even realized that amphibians were disappearing everywhere until
September 13 and 14, 1989, at the First World Congress of Herpetology, held
in Canterbury, England. Over the course of a two-day session on the conservation and management of species, presenters and attendees realized that
the same story kept repeating. "We had these great frogs." "They disappeared
a few years ago." "They're all gone." "I couldn't finish my research because
all my frogs disappeared." One after another, people traded stories of missing frogs and toads. The phrase "declining amphibians" was used for the
first time in a discussion chaired by C. Kenneth Dodd and Romulus Whitaker
on the afternoon of the 14th. Later the congress passed a resolution urging
governments worldwide to pay attention to the issue of dead, deformed and
dying frogs.

Frogs, pointed out the scientists, survived whatever it was that killed off
the last dinosaurs about 65 million years ago. They survived unimaginable
climate swings and sea-level fluctuations, from periods of no polar ice to
times when ice covered much of the Northern Hemisphere. They survived
volcanoes, floods, hurricanes and other natural disasters. But now some-
thing was killing the frogs worldwide. Researchers wanted to find out what

it was, and if the dying frogs had a message for their human neighbors.

While the numbers keep changing, at least five species of frogs are certainly extinct. Another 19, including some like the golden toad, *Bufo periglenes,* and the gastric brooding frog, *Rheobatrachus silus,* are probably also gone forever. Anecdotal reports put hundreds more frog species on the edge of extinction.

Some of the missing include species from agricultural areas, rainforests and deserts. The first species known to have become extinct in modern times disappeared in 1942. The list grows longer every year.

Perhaps the best-documented declines and losses are from Australia, where, of a total frog species count of 215, nine species are likely extinct. This represents a loss of 4 percent of their frog fauna over the past 20 years. Several other frog species are in great difficulty, and although the export of all Australian wildlife is strictly prohibited, it continues every day.

In an effort to ban the international trade in species considered at risk, more than 160 countries have signed the Convention on International Trade in Endangered Species of Wild Fauna and Flora (CITES). Legal trade is huge. Most frogs collected for the frog-leg trade are wild collected. In 1997 alone, the United Kingdom imported about 35,000 pounds (16,000 kg) of frog legs, which represents about one million frogs per year.

The U.K. figures pale besides import figures for the United States, which imported about 6.5 million pounds (3 million kg) of frog meat in each of the past two decades. This represents the deaths of about 90 million frogs just to satisfy the U.S. market. The illegal trade in amphibians for collectors and the pet trade will probably never be accurately documented.

Even with a nearly global ban on trade in these particular species, a web search for their names almost always turns up a commercial request or offer to trade. CITES claims that none of the listed species has been wiped out by trade; some have, however, disappeared as a consequence of other causes.

While some specialized frogs live in risky areas and are more likely to be wiped out in localized disasters like hurricanes, floods, landslides or volcanic eruptions, others merely have the misfortune to live in areas that humans developed or polluted with chemicals, metals and salts. Other frogs are at risk as a result of ozone layer thinning and radionuclides. The most poignant groups of disappearing frogs succumb to diseases and parasites brought about or encouraged by human activities. However, many experts now agree that most frog extinctions and reductions in population size are due more to human collecting and land-use changes including agriculture, industrialization and development. Introduced organisms – whether other frogs, insects, plants or higher vertebrates – all have an effect on their new ecosystems; some have been implicated in frog declines. Global warming may or may not affect all frogkind but some species will certainly be lost to its effects.

↑ Australian green treefrogs, *Litoria caerulea*, are usually green, but their name means "blue." For years, books have been suggesting the frog changed color in the preservative used to send it back to England. More recently, however, the unusually blue color phase has been photographed in the wild. These frogs are relatively common across a wide band of northern Australia, although some declines have been reported. This species is seen in the West in the pet trade, although legal export of all Australian frogs is strictly prohibited.

↑ A Pacific treefrog, *Pseudacris regilla*, backlit on a leaf in Washington state, U.S.

shown that even the most remote places on Earth are influenced by chemicals in rainfall and as particulates. Acidic water alone is not the problem, however. Given enough time, frogs can adapt even to highly acid conditions. One highly acidic habitat in southeast Queensland, Australia, is occupied by the acid-tolerant Cooloola sedge frog, *Litoria cooloolensis*. The water in its habitat is described as looking like a dark cup of tea.

Natural materials like dirt, metals and salts can cause trouble, too. Cutting forests causes erosion; the dirt released can choke breeding areas or cover habitat with layers of mud. Burning clear-cut waste increases carbon, sulfur and nitrogen oxides in the atmosphere, while the loss of canopy cover raises the temperature of remaining bodies of water. Increasing concentrations of soil salts due to agricultural irrigation change the alkalinity of water and soil. Many manufacturing processes release metals including mercury and lead. The effects of a few of these metals are well known, but even these few are inadequately studied. For example, selenium, the mineral

Survival Plan

The Mallorcan midwife toad, *Alytes muletensis,* offers a success story. The first specimen of this species was found as a fossil in 1977. The first live one was spotted in the wild in 1980. Five years later, the Durrell Wildlife Conservation Trust started a captive breeding program with 20 wild-caught toads. Several hundred have been released, and a breeding population is maintained in captivity on the Isle of Jersey in the English Channel. The Trust's public information points out that this species might be, "perhaps more appropriately named the midhusband toad," because the male carries the eggs wrapped around his hind legs until hatching.

which puts the "loco" in "locoweed," can cause severe developmental abnormalities in frogs at concentrations as low as two parts per million.

Even more chemicals are rearranged in the Earth's ecosystem by internal combustion engines, power plants and individual biomass burning. Carbon, which had been sequestered since before the time of the dinosaurs, has been burned and released as carbon dioxide and carbon monoxide. Unfortunately, coal, gas and petroleum are not pure carbon, hydrogen and oxygen. The impurities stored in fossil fuels as well as those added in the manufacturing process are all released as pollutants when burned for energy. Carbon dioxide concentration in the atmosphere has increased nearly 10 percent over the past one hundred years.

Studies on toxicity of various compounds on frogs rarely include more than one influence, and, like many such experiments, rarely do the frog any good at all as it dies in the end. These studies, called "LD50s" (lethal dose which kills 50 percent of the population), were very popular with a subset of herpetological graduate students. Occasional conferences still include some talks on how to kill half of your frogs while other sessions focus on how to conserve the few remaining frogs in a natural population.

← The edible frog, *Rana esculenta,* has been on the Old World menu since ancient times.

CFCs and Radiation

Releases of a group of chemicals called chlorofluorocarbons (CFCs) led to a thinning of the ozone layer, which is part of the Earth's atmosphere. In the 1970s, scientists realized that not only was the ozone layer thinning, but that an area with no ozone formed every winter over Antarctica – and is forming over the Arctic. Ozone is important because it helps to bounce ultraviolet light rays from the sun away from the surface of the Earth. Ultraviolet light is an ionizing radiation; it is used in industry to sterilize surfaces. Increasing ultraviolet light reaching the Earth's surface not only raises the rate of skin cancer in humans, but may also lead to genetic changes for other organisms. Research has shown that shading frog eggs in ponds from the increased ultraviolet helps the eggs to hatch out viable tadpoles.

It is surprising that despite the prevalence of radioactive power plants, fluids and hospital supplies around the globe, few have so far caused any major problems compared with fallout released by the open-air nuclear bomb testing that ended in 1963. Underground testing continued in both the former Soviet Union and the United States until September 1992, releasing radioactivity underground and, in some cases, contaminating groundwater. The direct effect of this testing on amphibians, as on most other organisms, is unknown.

U.S. nuclear tests on Bikini Atoll in the central Pacific Ocean in 1946 and the 1950s resulted in radioactive contamination of rainwater and pondwater. Frogspawn cultured in this water produced deformed frogs. Also

↓ At least eight enthusiastic male golden toads surround a female *Bufo periglenes*. The last member of this family was seen in the late 1980s.

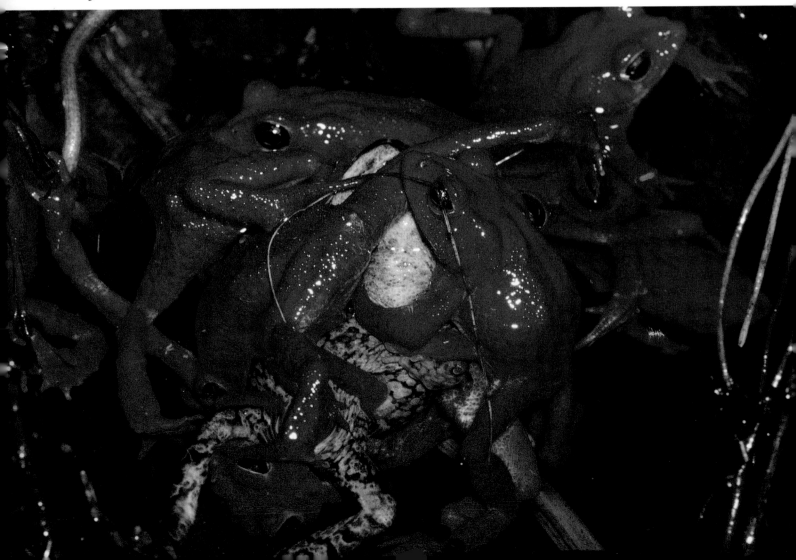

during the 1950s, deformed frogs were found in an Amsterdam wastewater canal that was draining a nuclear research institute.

Frogs from the appropriately named Radon Creek in Australia had high numbers of limb abnormalities. Other locations studied in connection with the Australian uranium mining industry have also shown a correlation between high levels of radioactivity and frog mutations.

On April 26, 1986, one of the nuclear power reactors near Kiev, in the former Soviet Union, released radioactivity that was first measured in Scandinavia. Days later, the Soviet government acknowledged the Chernobyl disaster. Continuing studies in the 30-kilometer (19-mile) zone centered on the failed reactor showed an initial 60 percent loss of fertility, but less apparent effects as time passed. U.S. nuclear testing at the Nevada test site alone released 10 times as much radiation into the environment as did the accident at Chernobyl.

Diseases

Until recently, relatively little was known about diseases in any amphibians except those of the clawed frogs, *Xenopus spp.,* and others kept commercially for food. Viral, bacterial, fungal and parasitic diseases can affect amphibians.

Viral diseases

Viral diseases of the family Iridoviridae are collectively called "ranaviruses" and have been reported from Asia, America, Europe and Australia. American bullfrogs, *Rana catesbeiana,* can be infected with tadpole edema virus while in California red-legged frogs, *Rana aurora,* are dying from the Redwood Creek ranavirus. In Croatia, a strain was cultured from edible frogs, *Rana esculenta,* and two more strains have been isolated in the United Kingdom – one from Ranid frogs, the other from Bufonid toads. American pigfrogs, *Rana grylio,* apparently are raised for food in China, where a specific ranavirus has been isolated from them. In the tadpole, ranavirus can cause 100 percent mortality. At some mass death sites, ranavirus and bacterial infections have been jointly blamed for the mortality.

Researchers continue to study some possibly unknown viruses in Australia which have led to the wasting death of many frogs. Other Australian researchers, meanwhile, are studying ranavirus to see if they can manufacture a "designer virus" to take out the cane toad, *Bufo marinus* – a major pest there. They express concern that their efforts might spread from the target to nontarget and perhaps even rare species, but research continues anyway.

Bacteria

Bacteria of many kinds infect frogs. Only a few are virulent. One bacteria, *Aeromonas hydrophila,* has wiped out whole communities of western toads as well as hundreds, perhaps thousands, of captive colonies of frogs worldwide. In the final stages of the infection, the frog's circulatory system breaks down and blood comes close to the surface of the skin, causing the classic "red-leg" appearance that precedes death. Frogs also get sick from *Chlamydia spp.* infections and can get tuberculosis from several bacterial agents.

Chytrid fungus

Fungi are far and away the biggest threat to global amphibian health, including *Saprolegnia, Mucor amphibiorum,* and *Batrachochytrium dendrobatidis,* called chytrid ("kit-rid") for short.

Chytrid fungus is responsible for chytridiomycosis, a fatal fungal disease that leads to thickening and sloughing of the skin and death by unknown causes. Its scientific name comes from the Central American poison frogs from which it was first cultured. After it was found, frogs that had been placed in museum collections were studied to see if historical data existed for the disease.

Researchers found that during the 20th century, clawed frogs, *Xenopus spp.,* were exported from their native South Africa in huge numbers to be used in human pregnancy testing as well as kept for pets and studied in laboratories around the world. Some frogs inevitably escaped or were released and established populations. In the wild, *Xenopus* carries chytrid without apparent damage to itself. Studies in South Africa show that chytrid is widespread in local populations and has been around since the 1930s and perhaps longer. It is now suspected that captive clawed frogs may be the source of the fungus that is decimating other frogs around the world.

Chytrid fungus does not kill infected tadpoles because only their mouthparts have keratin. The infection takes off when keratin forms elsewhere in the body during the complicated process of metamorphosis. The disease erupts in full force and wipes out the newly transforming frogs.

Massive metamorph mortality follows. Chytridiomycosis is fast-spreading and deadly. Chytrid spores can stay in infected water forever, even if the pond dries up and refills. Conservation authorities now plead with people not to move frogs around without first testing for chytrid fungus.

Genetic sequencing of chytrid specimens from all areas where the disease has been cultured has shown only a small amount of genetic variability. This leads researchers to conclude that chytridiomycosis is a recently emerged infectious disease that has been introduced into populations that have no resistance against it.

Two of the genetically closest samples were from Panama and Australia, which suggests that chytrid arrived in one country from the other. The U.S. wild strain seems to be slightly distant from those on other continents. As with many new diseases, chytrid is acting like a virulent pathogen wiping out everything in its path.

Global roundup

North America, Central America. The earliest known chytrid fungus was cultured from toads collected in 1974 in the Sierra Nevada Mountains. California thus has the dubious honor of having the first known outbreak of this emerging infectious disease. Shortly thereafter, in 1978, more infected frogs were found at the Savanna River Ecological Laboratory in South Carolina. Dead or infected frogs were found in Colorado in 1994, Illinois in 1996, Arizona in 1998 and North Carolina and Virginia in 2002. Chytrid from imported frogs has been known in the United States since the 1991 deaths of some Central American poison frogs. Specimens of chytrid-infected frogs were found in Mexico in 1983. Although infected frogs that had been imported from Central America were found in the United States in 1991, the first report of chytrid from Costa Rica was published in 1992 and from Panama in 1994.

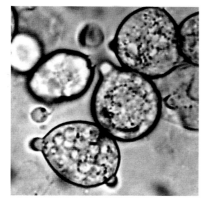

↑ Magnified, spores of chytrid look a little like any other cell, not the deadly killers they are.

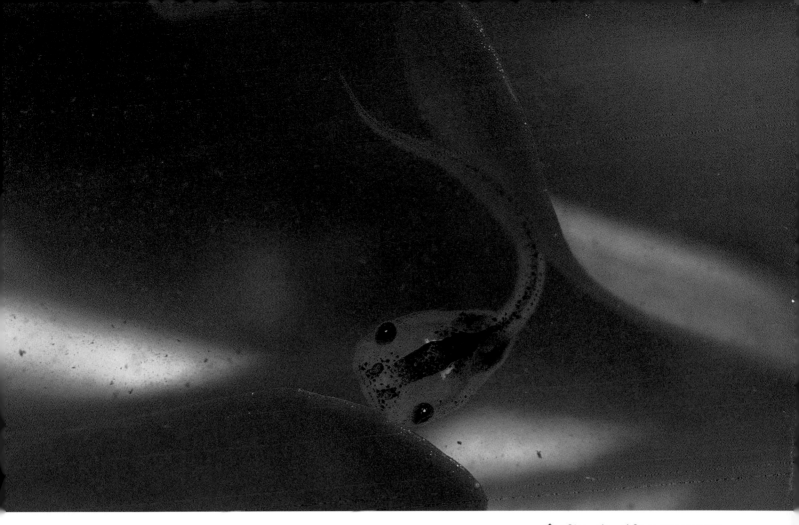

↑ African clawed frogs, *Xenopus spp.,* are asymptomatic carriers of chytrid fungus.

South America. The oldest chytrid-infected specimens in South America were found in Ecuador in 1980, then in Venezula in 1986. More than a decade later, in 1999, chytrid was found in Uruguay.

Europe. The first report of chytrid fungus in Spain was in 1997. Unfortunately, the fungus is now widespread in Spain, where it has been implicated with frog losses in a protected alpine park. The first reported chytrid fungus in Germany was found in a frog imported from Costa Rica in 1999. In 2001, an infected toad was found in Bologna, Italy.

Africa. Chytrid has been found in a clawed frog that died in 1938, making this the oldest infection on record. *Xenopus spp.* are now known to be asymptomatic carriers of chytrid fungus. West Africa reported its first chytrid specimen in 1998. At the same time, one was found in Kenya on the opposite side of the continent.

Oceania. The first known Australian chytrid was isolated from a specimen collected in 1978 from the east coast. It is now found in 46 species in both eastern and western portions of the continent. The last known member of one frog species, *Taudactylus acutirostris,* died of a chytrid infection in 1995 at the Royal Melbourne Zoological Gardens.

The first reports of chytrid in New Zealand were in 1999, when some introduced Australian frogs succumbed to the disease. By 2001, it had moved on to infecting endangered Archey's frogs, *Leiopelma archeyi.*

Asia. Only Asia remains without reports of chytrid fungus.

↑ Dainty green treefrog, *Litoria gracilenta*, calling from under a leaf in Australia.

Parasites

Several kinds of parasites infect frogs and toads. A well-studied nematode is implicated in midwestern U.S. frog deformities, and other parasites can cause wasting, pneumonia and death.

Nematode-caused frog deformities are not new. Studying preserved amphibians in museum collection revealed old specimens infected with the trematode *Riberiroia*, which spread rapidly in midwestern U.S. prairie ponds during the 1980s and 1990s. The number of infected places rose from nine historical locations to more than 50 hot spots in 2004.

Researchers suggest agricultural chemical nutrient runoff leads to more algae. More algae means more snails, which form an essential part of the trematode life-host cycle. More trematodes then attack the limb buds in tadpoles and cause deformed limbs to grow instead of normal ones. Some species have been wiped out at trematode-infested ponds. Researchers speculate that they make easy prey for birds and other predators, leading to localized extinctions.

Other parasites on frogs include *Capillaria* and many other nasty protozoans, all of which cause various syndromes, some of them fatal. Amphibian diseases in African clawed frogs, *Xenopus spp.,* are better known than those of frogs in general. African clawed frogs are the most used laboratory vertebrate on Earth, and so their maintenance in captivity is very important. There are even commercially available water treatments for red-leg and other frog bacteria aimed at the laboratory culture market.

Land-use Changes

The past 10,000 years have seen immense changes in Northern Hemisphere landscapes as the last of the continental glaciers retreated and meltwaters sculpted fertile glacial tills. About 5,000 years ago or more, agriculture began converting floodplains, grasslands and forests to human-managed environments. It wasn't until the beginning of the 19th century, however, with the rise of steam power, that humans had a major influence on their environment. The rise of commercial chemistry, the internal combustion engine and heavy equipment following the Second World War changed the landscape beyond all recognition.

Highways and railroad corridors now link every place on Earth. Roads penetrate the formerly most impenetrable places; tourists show up at the top and the bottom of the planet seeking wildlife and adventure. Roadkill numbers are immense. Frogs don't even have to be hit by a vehicle; the force of its passing can literally suck them inside out. Hundreds of flattened and inverted corpses line roadways on rainy nights.

Meanwhile, it seems that every square inch of industrialized area is paved over or built on. Any rain that falls on this armor-plated surface is whisked away into concrete-lined ponds and ultimately drained. Corporate headquarters are surrounded by acres of flat grass, planted on the ruins of the natural habitat bulldozed for the radiant city image.

Formerly diverse forests are logged, the remains burned or herbicided, and the land replanted in a monoculture of either trees or crops. During the time of the greatest-known amphibian declines, from 1978 to 1996, 12 percent of all the Amazonian rainforest was logged, an area of more than 200,000 square miles (500,000 square km). When the land loses fertility, it may be abandoned to second growth or developed further for industry or housing.

Midwestern U.S. prairies were long ago converted from the rich series of wetlands and dry spots into a marching monoculture of corn and soybeans, most of which are grown for cattle feed and ethanol. Too much agricultural fertilizer ended up in the ponds, fostering the growth of more pond plants and algae that consume all the oxygen in the water. This problem has caused die-offs in common frogs, *Rana temporaria*, in Europe during hibernation because the frogs are unable to get any oxygen from the water. Flood control projects resulted in channelized streams that cause water to flow off the land faster. This effectively reduces the amount of water available to frogs to breed. At the same time, ponds and wetlands of all types are deliberately drained to reduce the number of mosquitoes.

It's really simple. Drain the wetland or lower the water table and the pond is lost. When the pond is lost, the food is lost. With no food and no water, what's a frog to do?

Even before advancing human development encroached on them, ponds were lost to natural causes. It is the fate of all wet spots to become choked with silt and plants, eventually to become dry land. So frogs evolved to cope by moving from place to place in response to external conditions. What is different now is habitat fragmentation. Once a single population is lost, there may or may not be any frogs in the area to replace it. When a pond is lost, there may or may not be any new nearby ponds available for the remaining frogs to use.

In the early 1900s, a study found that the American toad, *Bufo americanus*, was the "most common amphibian in American cities." It fed on ants and insects and was often seen under dripping water pumps or breeding in horse troughs. As people changed from being an animal-powered to a machine-powered society, little wet spaces were drained, great piles of dung disappeared, mosquitoes were poisoned, and the frogs were lost.

Global Warming

Temperatures on Earth have fluctuated widely since frogs evolved somewhere around 200 million years ago. During the Mesozoic, global temperatures were from about 14 to 18°F (8 to 10°C) higher and carbon dioxide levels were three to four times as high as they are now.

Globally, cooling started about 35 million years ago at what we call the Eocene-Oligocene boundary as the climate entered its most recent glacial cycle. Earth is now in an interglacial cycle with warm temperatures and little continental ice. So frogs have lived through several cycles of both warmer and cooler times before.

What we are just beginning to understand is that a disaster for one species can be either a disaster or an opportunity for other species. We don't know which it will be until it happens. We don't know all the species of frogs that have ever lived on Earth; they don't fossilize well, and they aren't prestigious to study. So we don't know how many species rose and fell while the climate slowly changed and the continents moved over time. We do know we are losing frog species at an alarming rate as humans modify the environment. Some of the modifications initially seem beneficial; their negative consequences only appear later. This is the case with introduced species – those moved from their place of origin to a place in which they did not naturally occur.

Introduced Species

Some species seem to do well no matter where they end up. They are often called "supertramps" and are found in multiple new localities worldwide. Here are a few of the most widely distributed frog supertramps.

Marine or cane toads, *Bufo marinus*

Before the development of chemical insecticides, marine or cane toads, *Bufo marinus*, were introduced into at least 15 countries in an attempt to control a beetle, *Phyllophaga vandinei,* which ate sugarcane and other crops. In 1934 an article in *Nature* presented data showing that the toads had saved Puerto Rico's sugar fields. From Puerto Rico, they were introduced throughout the American tropics and into the Hawaiian islands, and from there to many other islands, including the Philippines. In 1935, 101 toads were released in Queensland, Australia. By 2003 they had spread widely from their original release site to an area that covered a half a million square kilometers (200,000 square miles) and are being blamed for damaging the beekeeping industry in Queensland and for the loss of many native animals that tried to eat these toxic toads.

It seems hard to believe that anyone ever sat down and counted each and every tiny black egg cased in clear jelly, but Australian researchers report that female cane toads lay from 8,000 to 25,000 eggs at a single time. It takes only a couple of days for the eggs to hatch into small, black tadpoles. The range of the cane toad is expanding rapidly.

Marine toads are incredibly hardy and adaptable. They can breed in sand ponds almost in the ocean and tolerate an amazing range of temperatures. In Florida, marine toads eat dog and cat food as well as insects. They are considered a major pest in Australia. Some people tolerate them; others kill every one they see. The cane toads just keep advancing.

Cuban treefrog, *Osteopilus septentrionalis*

Larger than most treefrogs, this species arrived in Florida from Cuba in 1931. They eat native frogs and utilize human-influenced and disturbed habitats better than the natives do. They have been blamed for power outages because they are drawn to the buzzing caused by transformers, and they sometimes cause a short circuit.

Clawed frogs, *Xenopus spp.*

Fully aquatic clawed frogs are some of the most widely distributed frogs on Earth. In the United States they have been found in Arizona, California, Colorado, Florida, Louisiana, Nevada, New Mexico, North Carolina, Virginia, Wisconsin and Wyoming.

↓ Marine toads, *Bufo marinus*, have spread by leaps and bounds in Australia since their deliberate introduction in 1935. They really don't eat cane beetles, but they do eat everything else and are toxic to just about everything that tries to eat them.

↑ California's native red-legged frog, *Rana aurora*, was first eaten by people, then other frogs. Finally its habitat is being lost to development as human populations grow.

They have been found to overwinter in water under ice in North Carolina, Virginia and Wisconsin. They tolerate both acid and alkaline waters and up to 40 percent sea water. Clawed frogs can estivate for up to eight months during drought and can survive a year without food.

Up until quite recently, clawed frogs were sold in "do-it-yourself frog kits" with no controls over the ultimate disposition of the adult animals. They may have been flushed, released or buried, or may still be alive in captivity.

Clawed frog colonies have also been found in the United Kingdom, Germany, the Netherlands and on remote Ascension Island in the South Atlantic. The frog is considered an invasive pest in Chile.

Of course, counting laboratory specimens, *Xenopus spp.* probably occur in every country that does any cell, molecular or developmental work. It is only a matter of time until more countries find clawed frogs on the loose.

Greenhouse frog, *Eleutherodactylus planirostris*

Greenhouse frogs most probably hitchhiked on tropical plants, arriving in Florida, Louisiana, Cuba, Jamaica, the Cayman Islands, the Bahamas, Veracruz in Mexico, and the state of Hawaii over the past 30 years. Greenhouse frogs have direct development from egg to frog, so they are not limited to areas with standing water to breed. They have recently been spotted on Guam, sparking fears that the coqui frog may not be far behind.

Coqui frog, *Eleutherodactylus coqui*

The greenhouse frog's close relative, the coqui frog, is native to the island of Puerto Rico but has established populations on several islands in the state of Hawaii. Things haven't gone well for coqui on Hawaii; the locals hate the noise and officials fear for endemic species. Studies have shown that caffeine, steam and citric acid sprays kill both Eleutherodactylids, and they are being used widely in the 50th state.

American bullfrog, *Rana catesbeiana*

Bullfrogs have been introduced around the world. Wherever they are found they exert a serious influence on the ecosystem as they munch their way through the local frog fauna as well as anything else small enough to fit into their mouths.

During the California Gold Rush of the 1850s, the local newly rich ate all the native red-legged frogs, *Rana aurora,* so they imported bullfrogs and started bullfrog farms. The bullfrogs escaped, of course, and started eating what was left of the red-legged frogs, which are now rare in the landscape where they were once common.

In the 1950s bullfrog farming started in Florida, but the bullfrogs rapidly escaped and started eating local animals including garter snakes, baby ducks and native birds. Bullfrogs have been introduced into the Caribbean and Europe as well as Asia.

5 Frogs in Myth & Culture

CHAPTER FIVE

Frogs in Myth & Culture

F ROGS REPRESENT TRANSFORMATION, death and rebirth in many cultures. Considering their amazing choruses, breeding groups, huge numbers of eggs and offspring, it is easy to see how early peoples would make the connection of frogs with fertility. The frog's connection with transformation comes from its extraordinary egg-to-tadpole-to-frog metamorphosis. In many transformation legends, the frog's companion is the only one to see past the spotted or slimy outer appearance and see the true beauty within. Frogs may have become a symbol of resurrection from their ability to remain dormant – looking nearly dead – and then come back to active life when conditions are right.

Myth arose from creative efforts to explain the world and describe historical events. Myth tends to deal with the doings of gods, supernatural beings, kings and armies. While tending to the details of daily life – drawing water, washing and bathing – people heard frogs calling and watched their exuberant mating and breeding. Much of the earliest frog art came from these observations, along with a liberal dose of allegory and imagination.

← A postcard from the early 1920s showing the Frog Prince.

←← Splendid leaf frog, *Agalychnis calcarifer.*

Myth & Culture

Sumer, Indus Valley and Egypt

The inhabitants of the lands between the Tigris and Euphrates rivers are credited with elaborate mathematics and astronomy, the use of wheeled vehicles and the first literature. Many of them lived in large, sophisticated cities and worshiped various anthropomorphic gods. Among the many other treasures of their world, Sumerians left us frog-shaped beads, called amulets, made of marble and other stones, each pierced to be worn on a cord.

Frogs are shown on cylinder seals, which Sumerians used as chops, or signature stones. Often nine frogs are shown, each frog representing one month of pregnancy. These seals may have been used as charts to help calculate the due date of the baby. Sumerians called frogs "bizaza." Translators note that "za" was considered a monotonous repeated noise, but a fragment of a Sumerian poem from about 3000 BCE tells a different tale. "The voice of the frog," it says, "is the glory of the marsh waters."

While the Sumerians and Egyptians left written records that we can read, the Indus civilization of Mohenjo-daro, Pakistan, transmitted its knowledge orally from 3000 to 1000 BCE. Poems and hymns are collected in the *Rig Veda*. In Book Seven, "Veda 103," credited to Vasishtha, frogs calling in a pond are compared to priests sitting around a bowl of an intoxicant called *soma*, endlessly repeating their prayers.

Some mycologists (people who study mushrooms) suggest that *soma* was a product of the fly-agaric mushroom associated with birch trees, also called a "toadstool." A study of the name of this fungus around the world shows an interesting pattern: French: *crapaudin*, "belonging to the toad"; Basque: *amoroto*, "the toad one"; Chinese: *hama chun*, "toad-mushroom."

Perhaps vague memories of *soma* have led to the connection between toads, toadstools and hallucinogens that persists to the present day.

Ancient Egypt had several parallel and intertwined myth traditions during the thousands of years that the culture inhabited the Nile Valley and controlled a region from Sudan to Syria. Egyptians called living frogs *kerer*, which was a reference to the sound of their call, and used the shapes of both frogs and tadpoles in hieroglyphic writing.

Among the earliest Egyptian myths, dating to about 3000 BCE, was one about four male frog-headed gods who, with their four female snake-headed consorts, created the world. One of the eight, Amun, later became the chief god of Egypt. Another of the eight, Heh, was shown with either a frog head or a human head. He was the god of infinity and time; his symbol, with the arms upraised, indicates one million, considered equal to eternity.

A magnificent pectoral necklace that once belonged to Princess Sithatho-ryunet was found in her tomb at Lahun. It is now in the Metropolitan Museum of Art in New York City. The royal-name cartouche rests on the one million sign of the god Heh with his arms upraised. Hanging from Heh's elbow is "hefner," the tadpole, a hieroglyphic sign for 100,000. The blessing thus hopes for perpetual life for eternity, hedged by 10 percent!

The goddess of childbirth and fertility, Heqet, was shown with a frog's head and had the frog character in her name. In the pyramid texts at Dendera, in the funeral of Osiris panel, Heqet is represented by a frog symbol shown at the feet

↑ This ivory wand was used to assist a birth near Thebes around 2000 to 1700 BCE. Decorated with the head of Anubis and Heqet's toad, *Bufo viridis.*

of the mummified god. Other texts describe how Heqet assisted every day with the birth of Ra, the sun, from the underworld in which it spent the night. Perhaps her inclusion at the funeral is as a symbol of resurrection. Unwrapped mummies have revealed Heqet amulets tucked in the layers of linen.

Frog-shaped amulets to Heqet were made by the thousands and knives decorated with a frog's head were laid on pregnant women to protect them. Curiously, the earliest amulets are toad shaped and probably represent an inflated *Bufo viridis.* Later the amulets become more frog-like, perhaps representing *Rana mascariensis.* In both cases, Egyptologists who study such things think they represent the human embryo and developing fetus.

In the second through fourth centuries CE, oil lamps in the shape of stylized frogs were common in Egypt, Greece and Rome. One terra-cotta lamp, found in Thebes, was inscribed, "I am the resurrection." Coptic Christians carved a frog into the catacombs in Alexandria and their incredible subterranean stone churches in Ethiopia.

Crete, Greece and Rome

Paintings on Cretan storage jars dated to about 2000 BCE show frogs or toads with a sign believed to represent the womb. In common with other early cultures, the early Greeks associated frogs with fertility and human reproduction.

The blind poet Homer is credited with the short composition *Batrachomyomachia (The Battle of Frogs and Mice)*, around 800 BCE. In it Athena, the goddess of war, gives her reason for not taking the side of the frogs: "Once, when I was returning early from war ... very tired, and though I wanted to

↑ A Roman vase decorated with toads is in the Louvre Museum, Paris. Pots remarkably similar to it are sold in garden stores today.

sleep, the [frogs] would not let me even doze a little for their outcry; and so I lay sleepless with a headache until cock-crow," complained the goddess.

The only remaining Greek comedies from the 5th century BCE were written by Aristophanes (448–380 BCE). In *The Frogs*, the god Dionysus descends to the underworld. As he is rowed across the River Styx to the land of the dead, Hecate's frogs begin to sing. Their refrain, "Brekekekex koax koax" sounds like the repeated calls made by frogs in breeding season.

The Greek writer Aesop lived about 400 BCE. His oft-quoted *Fables* were not intended for children, but as political statements for adults. Aesop uses frogs in one of his most famous fables, "The Frogs Desiring a King," to illustrate the point that you should be careful of what you want; otherwise, you simply may receive what you don't expect.

The Romans assimilated gods, myths and legends from all corners of their empire. They used Egyptian frog lamps and made their own frog-themed bronze weights, fountain bases and garden sculptures. When Rome collapsed and its empire reformed under Christian princes, much of what had been accepted and cherished was turned into heresy, witchcraft and anathema. *The Book of Revelation*, written early in the Christian Era, typifies the spirit of the times. Verse 16:13 reads, "And I saw three unclean spirits like toads come out of the mouth of the dragon, and out of the mouth of the beast, and out of the mouth of the false prophet."

Asia

Chinese culture is as old as that of Sumer, the Indus Valley and Egypt. Many Chinese legends refer to a fungus growing from the forehead of a toad as the secret of immortality. In one legend, a woman named Chang O stole the Elixir of Immortality from her husband and fled to the moon. There she met the rabbit who prepared ingredients for the immortality potion. Chang O was changed into a three-legged toad and forced to stay on the moon. But her husband took pity on her and built her a jade palace on the side of the moon that cannot be seen from Earth. He lives on the Sun, so he can visit her only at new moon when the sun shines on Chang O's palace. The toad's three legs refer to the three lunar phases, and it is said that eclipses happen when the toad tries to swallow the moon.

To this day, Chinese people point out both the rabbit and the three-legged toad on the face of the full moon. They celebrate the Moon Festival at the full moon that people in the West call the harvest moon. In an interesting parallel to ancient Western legend, the toad also controls the dark part of Earth's year, what the Chinese consider the yin half. Offerings to the moon at the festival include pomegranates and other moon-shaped fruits, moon cakes, and carved melons that look rather like fleurs-de-lis.

During the Han Dynasty, from 206 BCE to 220 CE, a beautiful seismograph was manufactured to identify for the emperor the part of his tectonically active nation that had experienced an earthquake. When an earthquake occurred, a ball dropped from the mouth of one of eight dragons on the side of the device, landing in the mouth of the toad below it. The emperor could

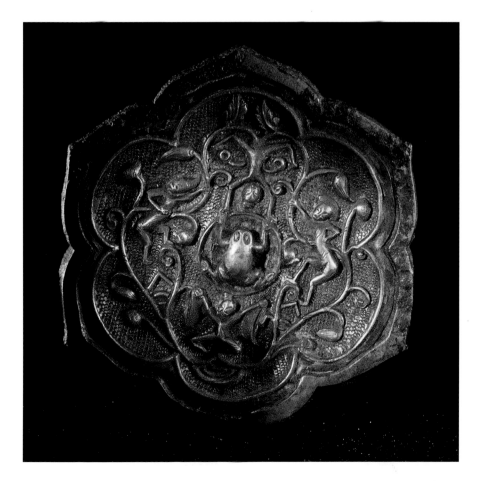

← The toad in the center of this unusual six-sided Tang Dynasty (618–970 CE) bronze mirror is surrounded by four playful monkeys. Small mirrors like this one were made to be worn from a cord and were given as awards, love tokens and wedding presents.

→ Frogs have been associated with rain in many cultures. This print by Japanese-Canadian artist Naoko Matsubara is simply entitled *Rain*.

then send help to the afflicted area before being asked.

The first known compasses used magnetized "mysterious tadpoles" that spun around on their bases until their tails pointed south, toward the positive magnetic pole. It is said that the armies of the Khans used lodestone tadpoles in their cooks' woks to guide the course of their conquest.

Liu Hai, a real minister in 10th-century Chinese government, was transformed into a character of myth. He was pictured as a Taoist magician with a three-legged toad companion that could carry him wherever he wanted to go. Since toad toxins were used in Chinese medicine, it is possible to see how Liu Hai could fly around on the back of a toad. One of the stories says that the three-legged toad was in a well, poisoning the water because he could not get out. Farmers had unsuccessfully tried everything to dislodge the toad. Then Liu Hai coaxed the toad out using a string of five gold coins with square-cut holes in the middle. Since the creature liked money so much, the three-legged toad became a symbol of prosperity. Statuettes were made during the Ching dynasty in the 19th century and are still being manufactured in southern China and southeast Asia. Even today, these "three-legged toads" can be purchased for use in household Feng Shui and prosperity ceremonies.

Folk religion in India occasionally has elaborate marriage ceremonies for frogs in an effort to call the rains. People dress and paint the "bride and groom," have a lovely wedding and release the frogs afterward.

The spread of Buddhism from India to China and Japan brought a new series of frog legend and myth into the culture of the region. In one story, a frog who chose not to interrupt the teachings of Buddha was reborn in the realm of the gods as the great god, Lord Indra.

In Japan, a famous temple, Tsukubasan Jinja, is toad-shaped. Every year on the first Sunday of August, vendors compete with each other at the Mount Tsukuba Gama Matsuri Toad Festival in Japan. Each vendor claims his or her product is made from special toads and protects the wearer from many evils.

Indonesia and Australia

Indonesian wood carvings of flying frogs represent the frog legend of a little frog who told himself he could fly over and over, until one day he found he really could fly. Indonesia, of course, has a real gliding frog (*Rhacophus pardalis*), which may be the inspiration for the legend.

In Bali, gamelan musicians playing in the rice paddies and along roads try to call down the rains by getting the frogs to croak.

Australian Aboriginals, using a hollow tubed instrument called a didgeri-doo, play frog sounds as well as original compositions based on frog-related dreamtime themes. Aboriginal people believe frogs can bring rain, and that the calls of frogs indicate rain is on the way.

Aztec, Inca and Mayan

In Aztec MesoAmerica, Tlaltecuhti or Tlaltecuhtli, a giant toad or toad-goddess, represented an endless cycle of death and resurrection. She was sometimes shown giving birth to the new world while swallowing the souls of the dead. Her mouth was a cave to the underworld.

For the Inca of South America, toads not only represented the rains and fertility, but also were noted for their ability to live on land and in water. Toads are featured in Inca weavings and presumably in their legends and myths, unfortunately lost at the time of the Spanish conquest.

Chaac, the Mayan rain god, was often considered a four-part god: one specially colored Chaac ruled the winds of each of the four compass directions. Artistically, Chaac is shown with a frog and a thunder axe. Tears coming from his eyes represent rain. Priests of Chaac may have used special frog-shaped whistles to make calls either for worship purposes or to encourage the local frogs to call and start the rains. Farmers in the otherwise Christianized Yucatán Peninsula of Mexico still pray to Chaac for rain.

Dozens of reliefs and sculptures of Chaac are seen throughout the Yucatán Peninsula. His hooked nose often extends off the corners of buildings.

A Mayan story saved by the weavers who have passed along the design tells how the toad sung at the entrance of the Earth Lord's mountain cave while his daughters combed cotton. Thunder then transformed the cotton into clouds that bring rain to the people.

The toad glyph was used as one of the 20 day-name symbols, and a toad sign was used to denote the ascension of a new ruler. In one Mayan legend, "little brother toad" on Earth sings and dances in the rain to encourage "big brother toad" in heaven to send the rains.

The endangered Panamanian golden frog is a revered and popular symbol in the Republic of Panama. It is believed that anyone who sees a golden frog gets good luck. Gold and clay pre-Columbian frog-shaped artifacts, called huacas, are sought and treasured by archaeologists and collectors. The bright-yellow coloring of the frog is a potent warning, too. Researchers have isolated what they describe as unique neurosensitive tetrodotoxin from these frogs.

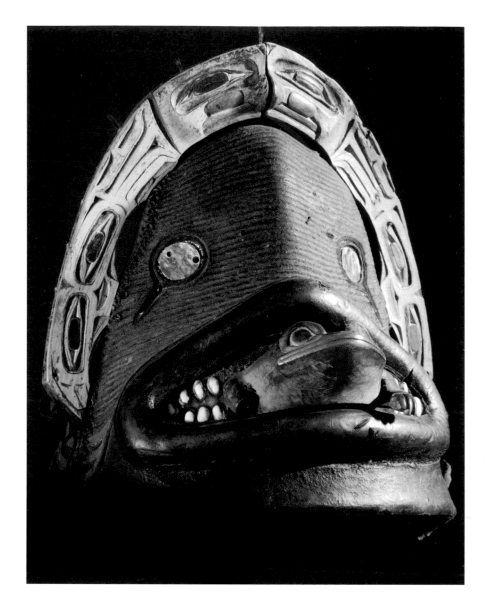

→ A defensive Tlingit headpiece portraying a ground shark with a frog in its mouth was crafted of wood, leather and abalone shell along the northwest coast of North America probably during the 19th or 20th centuries.

Tlingit

Raven was the creator god of the Tlingit people of coastal British Columbia and Alaska. In part of the creation stories, Raven asks Frog to get him some sand from the bottom of the ocean. Frog gets Raven to agree to be keeper of Earth's treasures, then uses an old skin to gather up sand. Raven sprinkles the sand around the Earth, and dry land appears where formerly there was only ocean.

Europe

During the Middle Ages in Europe, from about 500 to 1500 CE, there were many superstitions and prejudices about the natural world and its creatures, including frogs and toads. Toads and everything they touched were considered deadly poisonous. Giovanni Boccaccio (1313–75) composed *The Decameron* between 1349 and 1351. It is a series of tales; one tells how two lovers died after touching leaves of sage to their mouths. During the trial, the judge ordered the garden searched:

FROGS

> For, just in the middest of the bed, and at the maine roote, which
> directed all the Sage in growth, lay an huge mighty Toad, even weltring
> (as it were) in a hole full of poyson; by meanes whereof, in conjecture
> of the judge, and all the rest, the whole bed of Sage became
> envenomed, occasioning every leafe thereof to be deadly in taste. None
> being so hardy, as to approach neere the Toade, they made a pile of
> wood directly over it, and setting it on a flaming fire, threw all the Sage
> thereinto, and so they were consumed together.

A mystical jewel called the toadstone, bufonite or crapandina was supposed to be found in the center of a toad's forehead. This jewel was believed to warn its wearer of the presence of poison. In 1579 Thomas Lupton published a book called *A Thousand Notable Things*, in which he provided instructions on how to remove the toadstone from the toad:

> Put a great or overgrowne tode into an earthen potte, and put the same
> into an antes hyllocke, & cover the same with earth, which tode at
> length antes wyll eate, so that the bones of the toad and [toad]stone wyll
> be left in the potte.

Toads were considered the familiars of witches, who were often known by the alleged mark of a toad's foot on their shoulder. Witches reportedly used the toad both as the sacrifice of the black mass and to prepare what were called "flying ointments." During the Middle Ages, midwives were considered followers of Hecate, the Queen of the Witches. An earlier, less prejudiced culture had considered midwives helpers of Heqet, the frog fertility goddess in Ancient Egypt.

In this recipe for disaster from *Macbeth* (1611), the three witches conjure Hecate. "Sweltered venom" refers to toad toxin:

> For a charm of powerful trouble,
> Like a hell-broth boil and bubble ...
> Toad, that under cold stone
> Days and nights has thirty-one
> Swelter'd venom sleeping got,
> Boil thou first in the charmed pot ...
> Eye of newt and toe of frog,
> Wool of bat and tongue of dog.

In addition to this stirring spell, William Shakespeare (1564–1616), in his various plays, included more than two dozen negative references to frogs and toads.

Even during this long period of prejudice, frogs were still considered good fertility symbols and people left frog statuettes and bits of metal, including coins, at springs as offerings to these spirits. Gypsy legends insist that the Queen of the Fairies lives in a golden castle shaped like a toad.

Carrying a dried toad was considered a form of protection against the plague, and just seeing a toad could mean the end of a drought, a long and happy marriage, or general good fortune. The frog and toad also represented resurrection and redemption. Frogs were considered the spirits of unborn children, and killing them could bring misfortune. The tales that would be recorded as "The Frog Prince," while dating to at least Roman times, were continually passed along and embellished during this era.

And, of course, people always go with what seems to work best. An annual toad-fair was held in Dorsetshire, England, where local healers sold charms and medicines. In later years, traveling "toad-doctors" went door-to-door hawking their potions.

Printing and other influences ended the Middle Ages with a surge of interest in the outside world we call the Renaissance and Age of Discovery. Leonardo da Vinci (1452–1519) experimented on frogs. In 1487 da Vinci went in search of what he called "the foundation of movement and life" by attempting to find out if it was the head, the heart, the bowels, or the spinal cord and brain that were essential to life. He determined that the brain controlled all the other organs. It was the first known recorded scientific experiment on frogs, and marks the beginning of their importance to science and medicine.

Finally, attitudes toward frogs and toads started to relax and they began to be seen at least sympathetically, if not as a source of humor. Nicholas Chamfort (1741–94) wrote, "Swallow a toad in the morning if you want to encounter nothing more disgusting the rest of the day." But old attitudes die hard. Even today, Wicked Witches are green!

Some Classic Legends

SOME FROG LEGENDS and stories are as old as the oldest frog myths and can be divided into three general types: (1) frog prince or princess stories; (2) frog trickster stories; and (3) other frog stories.

The most familiar frog legend is the story of the prince or princess who is magically changed into a frog and needs someone to help break the spell so he or she can return to human form. We can tell that the frog prince story was common, at least in Rome, before the birth of Christ. Around 100 BCE Publilius Syrus, the oft-quoted Latin writer, commented, "We are born princes and the civilizing process makes us frogs." Variations on the "frog prince" story are found around the world – from Korea, Japan and China through Asia and the Middle East; then into Europe, and from there to its colonies and trading partners.

In the Kootenai Native American legend, *How the Frog Won the Race*, frogs are described as slow runners but fast thinkers. Antelope was chief of a village uphill from the village of the frogs and the fastest runner around. One day the chief of the frogs challenged Antelope to a race. Antelope was sure he would win because frogs can only hop; but the frog said he could think fast even if he ran slowly – and bet all his people's frog skins that he would win. Antelope bet everything his people owned because he was sure he would win the frog skins. These would keep his people warm in winter and cool in summer.

Chief Frog was a trickster, though. Knowing that all frogs look the same to Antelope, he placed his people one hop apart along the race course and told them to hop, one at a time, always ahead of Antelope – who would never be able to tell that he was racing different frogs. The chief hopped first, then all his people hopped one after another, always ahead of Antelope. Antelope arrived back in his village behind the frog, losing both the race and everything his people owned.

Some Celebrated Frogs

MARK TWAIN WAS the pseudonym used by Samuel Langhorne Clemens (1835–1910), a gifted newspaperman and writer whose literary career began with the 1867 publication of *The Celebrated Jumping Frog of Calaveras County*. A frog-jumping event is now held every year in Angel's Camp, California, in honor of Twain's story.

Toads can still be seen as a little off the edge. Kenneth Grahame (1859–1932) wrote the stories that would become *The Wind in the Willows* (1908) for his young son, whose behavior was reportedly the inspiration for the nutty antics of Mr. Toad of Toad Hall who cries:

> Ho, ho! I am the Toad, the motor car snatcher, the prison breaker, the Toad who always escapes. Sit still, and you shall know what driving really is, for you are in the hands of the famous, the skillful, the entirely fearless Toad!

The American poet Emily Dickinson (1830–86) wrote short poems about frogs in natural habitat and, as in this untitled work, used them as metaphors for human behavior:

↑ Mark Twain's tall tale about the celebrated frog of Calaveras County marked the start of his literary career.

I'm Nobody! Who are you?
Are you – Nobody – Too?
Then there's a pair of us?
Don't tell! they'd advertise – you know!

How dreary – to be – Somebody!
How public – like a Frog –
To tell one's name – the livelong June –
To an admiring Bog!

Perhaps the most celebrated amphibian of modern times, Kermit the Frog, was created by Jim Henson (1936–1990) from a green coat and a couple of Ping Pong balls when Henson was still in school. Kermit first went on NBC's adult interview *Tonight Show* in 1957, appeared on PBS' award-winning educational program, *Sesame Street*, as an interviewer of nursery rhyme characters in the early 1970s and again after 2001. In the late 1970s and 1980s he and a cast of Henson characters starred in *The Muppet Show*, appeared in BBC specials and several movies. Giving rise to his frog voice, Kermit has crooned several hits including, "It's Not Easy Being Green." Kermit has addressed college graduation classes and was awarded a star on the Hollywood Walk of Fame. He gave an eloquent elegy at Henson's funeral and appeared at Queen Elizabeth's Jubilee Concert in 2002. A statue of Henson and Kermit stands on the campus of their alma mater, The University of Maryland, College Park.

Urban Legends

Frogs appear in several urban legends, all definitely not true. One says that if you put a frog in boiling water, it will hop right out; but if you put a frog in cool water and bring it to a boil, it will stay in and get cooked. Actual experimentation has proved the opposite, but the story continues to circulate. Another urban legend series claims consumers found frogs in various containers, from bags of frozen peas to fast food. A third group of potentially dangerous urban legends appears to condone toad-licking. Some versions even give recipes quite reminiscent of Middle Ages alchemy.

Humor and Cartoons

"Analyzing humor is like dissecting a frog," wrote E.B. White (1899–1985). "Few people are interested and the frog dies of it."

Frog jokes are modern fables. The uses of frogs and toads in modern humor are limitless.

An engineering student found a frog who promised to turn into a beautiful princess if he would kiss her. Instead he put the frog in his pocket. Every day he'd take it out and the frog would beg and plead for the kiss so she could turn into a beautiful princess. Finally, she pleaded with him to tell her why he wouldn't kiss her and release the enchantment. He explained, "I'm almost at graduation and don't have time for a girlfriend, but a talking frog is cool!"

A psychic tells a frog, "You will meet a beautiful young woman who wants to know everything about you." The frog is excited and asks the psychic where he will meet her. The psychic replies, "In Biology 101 lab."

↑ One in a series of memorable and creative television commercials is eerily reminiscent of the ancient *soma* priests mumbling over their intoxicants. Here three frogs sit around a swamp, monotonously chanting the name of the beer.

Michigan J. Frog

Michigan J. Frog was created in 1955 by cartoonist Chuck Jones for his animated short film, *One Froggy Evening*. He's a singing-and-dancing frog – but only when no one is looking. Warner Brothers Television uses the dapper Michigan J. as its network logo and spokesfrog.

Ally McBeal

A character in an episode of the television program *Ally McBeal* aired on November 9, 1998, had a pet frog named "Steven" until one night some poorly written kitchen instructions to "feed the frog" were misinterpreted and he was made into an appetizer. Animal rights activists immediately protested.

Frogs are so much a part of modern Western culture that the thought of a beautiful woman kissing a frog is not merely acceptable, but it's been done. In that vein, Cameron Diaz, actress and the voice of enchanted green Princess Fiona in *Shrek*, summed up the long and strange journey of frogs in myth when she said, "I'd kiss a frog even if there was no promise of a Prince Charming popping out of it. I love frogs."

Epilogue

ALL IS NOT LOST FOR FROGS. All may be lost for some frogs, but other frogs are – as they have been for millions of years – on the move and expanding their range. People now understand the importance of frogs in the ecosystem. Once considered ugly, horrible and malignant animals, frogs are now seen as indicators of environmental health and symbols of natural balance.

This may be as false a view as the ancient superstitions we now find so amusing. Nature is not ever "in balance." If it were, the continents would be covered with climax communities each in its own clearly defined area. No community would ever intrude upon another and upset the balance. Nature is unbalanced because Nature is random. Events have no memory, say the statisticians; events can happen or not happen for a reason or for no reason. And events are rarely, if ever, predictable. That is why Nature is described as "stochastic" – random events happening randomly, producing what can be made to appear like an ordered structure.

The frogs know none of this of course. Their world is to them as it has been to their ancestors since their time began – a place to hatch, eat, transform, eat, mate, eat and die. Random events that happen to a single frog may be of great importance to its life or death; only vast aggregations of random events produced the Earth as it was. And only random events will produce the Earth as it will be.

Randomly some frogs will become extinct; others will expand their ranges. As the latter group become isolated in new habitats, speciation may occur. Or the frogs may be wiped out in stochastic events. It is Nature. One never knows.

← True toads, such as this American toad, *Bufo americanus*, are survivors. They can breed in tire ruts, live far from water and overwinter in the frozen north. Whether frogs or their descendants – individually or in aggregate – can adapt to life with more than six billion humans on Earth remains to be seen.

↑ Female marsupial frogs, *Gastrotheca spp.*, carry their eggs in special dorsal pouches, through the tadpole phase and until the young hatch out. Much of their native Venezuelan habitat has been lost to human land use changes.

What is different now is the human hand. The acts of human beings are not random. Recovery does not occur in one place as destruction occurs in another. Even when not wiped out completely by disease or pollution, populations are divided by fields, roads and towns, preventing recolonization after losses.

Humans are beginning to take responsibility for species survival. There are species survival plans for many endangered frogs, and scientists continue to search the world, both for new frogs and for the missing. Organizations have been formed, both to share knowledge and to attempt to preserve frogs in the wild and learn more about them in captivity.

Careful and patient fieldwork continues to pay off. A new family of frog was discovered in the Indian Ghats in 2003, and more than 100 species of frogs new to science were discovered in a careful survey of the island of Sri Lanka. One of the researchers found a new species of frog in his own backyard and was quoted as saying that one should never forget to look close to home as well as far away.

In 2003, several individual Rancho Grande harlequin frogs, *Atelopus cruciger,* of different ages were discovered hopping around by a botanist doing some research in a northern Venezuelan rainforest. They had been described as missing since 1996 and were presumed extinct. The botanist is getting a group together to go back to look for more.

Individual efforts can add up to meaningful benefits for frogs and toads. Gardening for amphibians often gives individual frogs needed habitat for feeding, estivating and hibernating, while road tunnels and road closures reduce mortality during breeding season. Individual homeowners could

← Maki frog, *Phyllomedusa lemur;*
Monte Verde Cloud Forest, Costa
Rica

reduce or eliminate their use of toxic products around the home and garden.
Captive-breeding frogs and toads and releasing the offspring in the wild, if
done with sensitivity to genetics, diseases and legal restrictions, may be the
salvation of some species.

Even simple changes can make a huge difference. Encouraging computer-
ized, virtual dissections instead of the real thing at most levels of education,
or using species considered pests instead of wild-caught adult animals, can
reduce collection stress on native frogs and toads. Australia might consider
a new industry – exporting wrapped, chilled cane toads, *Bufo marinus,* as
high school and college dissection specimens.

Most importantly, a profound desire to preserve frogs for future generations is probably their best hope for survival. Individuals can perform
random acts of survival and consider the effects of their actions on Nature.
Frogs and toads have proven over the vast span of geological time that they
are successful, adaptable and persistent. Given half a chance and a little habitat they will continue to sing sweetly on rainy nights for millions of years to
come.

Frog Miscellany

Natural History & Anatomy

Oldest fossil

The oldest fossil frog is called *Vieraella herbsti*. It was found in early Jurassic sediments in Patagonia, Argentina, and dates between 188 and 213 million years old.

Newest family

Researchers announced the discovery of a new family of frogs in October 2003. The only known species in the family was found in remote mountains in southern India and was named *Nasikabatrachus sahyadrensis*. All the other frog families were discovered and named in the 18th and 19th centuries.

Newest species

About 70 species of frogs are discovered every year, so the holder of this honor is subject to change at any time.

Most toxic frog

The golden dart frog, *Phyllobates terribilis,* is often credited with producing "the most toxic naturally occurring substance," called tetradotoxin. In captivity, where they are not eating their native food items, dart frogs lose their toxicity.

Most toxic toad

The dubious honor of most poisonous toad belongs to the giant marine or cane toad, *Bufo marinus*.

← Weighing a Goliath frog, *Conraua goliath*, Cameroon, Africa.

Largest frog

The biggest frog in the world is the Goliath frog, *Conraua goliath*, found in Cameroon, Africa. It can weigh up to 8 pounds (3.6 kg) and grow to 35 inches (89 cm) long.

The largest frog in North America is the American bullfrog, *Rana catesbeiana*, which can weigh 4 pounds (1.8 kg) and grow to 12 inches (30 cm) long.

Largest toad

The world's biggest toad is the marine toad, or cane toad, *Bufo marinus*, weighing in at 6 pounds (2.7 kg) and measuring 21 inches (54 cm) long.

Smallest frog

The smallest frog in the Southern Hemisphere is the gold frog, *Psyllophryne didactyla*. Its tiny body measures only about ⅜ of an inch (9.5 mm).

The smallest frog in the Northern Hemisphere was discovered in 1996 and named *Eleutherodactylus iberia* in honor of Mount Iberia, Cuba, where it was found. It also measures a tiny ⅜ of an inch (9.5 mm) from snout to vent.

Most prolific

A single female cane toad, *Bufo marinus*, can lay from 30,000 to 35,000 eggs.

Furthest north

The European Common frog, *Rana temporaria*, lives near the northernmost point in Europe at about 71 degrees North; the moor frog, *Rana arvalis*, lives at 69 degrees North near Murmansk in the former Soviet Union.

The wood frog, *Rana sylvatica*, is the only frog that lives north of the Arctic Circle in the New World. Wood frogs hibernate through extremely cold winters by changing their body fluids into a form of antifreeze. This keeps their cells from freezing and exploding from the expansion of the cell water. Even a wood frog's fertilized eggs can overwinter through a full freezing cycle and resume development when the weather warms.

Furthest south

In 1839 Charles Darwin reported seeing a frog at 50 degrees South latitude, but none were known south of there in Tierra del Fuego on account of the extreme nature of the environment. In 1903 the government of Argentina set aside a national park that contains the habitat of Darwin's frog, *Rhinoderma darwinii*, locally called the "ranita del Chalhuaco" after the valley in which it lives, as well as the habitat of another local frog, the Patagonian frog, *Atelognathus nitoi*. The southernmost toad, *Bufo variegatus*, lives at the southernmost tip of South America at 52 degrees South latitude.

Antarctica

Antarctica has no living frogs. It may have frog fossils because it has dinosaur-age sedimentary deposits.

Biggest mouth

Algae-feeding tadpoles can open their mouths 180 degrees, more than any other kind of vertebrate animal.

Clawed toes

African clawed frogs of the genus *Xenopus* are the only frogs in the world with claws; the three outer toes are tipped with keratin.

Flying frog

There are two frogs called "flying frogs," the Reinwardt's flying frog, *Rhacophorus reinwardtii*, and Wallace's flying frog, *Rhacophorus nigropalmatus*. Both frogs really glide downward rather than fly.

Glue frog

Males of the genus *Breviceps* from southern Africa have such short front legs that they can't grasp and hold the female to breed. They use special skin secretions to glue themselves onto the females.

Hairy frog

The hairy frog of Cameroon, *Trichobatrachus robustus,* doesn't have real hair. Instead, it is covered in tiny blood vessels that look like hair. These vessels help the frog get more oxygen out of the water, especially during breeding season, when the frogs need a faster metabolism.

Live-bearing

The Puerto Rican live-bearing frog, *Eleutherodactylus jasperi,* was discovered in 1976. Unfortunately it was considered extinct by 2003.

The Mount Nimba live-bearing toad, *Nectophrynoides occidentalis,* was discovered by a 21-year-old explorer in Guinea. The toads used to occur in the Ivory Coast and Liberia as well as in Guinea. However, concern about its continued survival is high. Nimba toads mate by cloacal contact, which results in internal fertilization. Females live underground for the first six months after fertilization. During this time, their offspring grow slowly; the rate accelerates in the last trimester, when the females resume activity. The females deliver between two and 16 live toads nine months after fertilization.

Lungless

The Titicaca water frog, *Telmatobius culeus,* breathes through its baggy skin because it has no lungs.

Teeth

The South American marsupial frog, *Amphignathodon guentheri,* is the only frog with real teeth in its lower jaw.

Tongueless frog

The African clawed frog, *Xenopus laevis,* has no tongue.

Attack of the Teargassing Toads

One night after a herp meeting a prominent colleague and I went road hunting along the U.S.–Mexico border. We found absolutely nothing except dozens of border officers who backed off at my friend's high-level Fish and Wildlife identification and one Couch's spadefoot toad, *Scaphiopus couchii*. It was drizzling, and I brought the toad into the car for a good identification. We were paging through the field guide and put on the defoggers to clear the windows when we were overcome by a wave of noxious vapor emitted by the toad. It was like teargas and we exploded out of the car, put the toad in a ditch and tried to air out the car. Whatever toxin the toad let loose that night, I was down for 24 hours sleeping with runny eyes and all the symptoms of a major cold. My colleague was similarly affected. Other reports of noxious fumes from southwestern toads have been reported. Ever since, in an effort to make light of a miserable experience, I've called that switch on my dashboard my "de-frogger." – E.B.

Vegetarian frog

Plant material accounts for nearly 80 percent of the diet of the Indian green frog, *Rana hexadactyla*. It is the only known leaf-eating frog.

Saltwater

Southeast Asian crab-eating frogs, *Rana cancrivora,* live in mangrove swamps in brackish or near-marine conditions by changing their body fluid chemistry to become osmotically in balance with seawater. They grow up to 3 inches (8 cm) long.

Science and Technology Records

Barometers

Until electronic instruments became common, people in parts of rural Germany kept green treefrogs, *Hyla arborea,* in tall bottles with wide necks. The bottles were half full of water and there was a ladder leading from the water to the top of the bottle. In fair weather, the frogs climbed to the top, but when it was going to rain, they climbed back down toward the water.

Earliest experiment

Leonardo da Vinci (1452–1519) performed the first recorded frog experiment in 1487, when he discovered that the brain controlled all the other organs.

Electricity

A green frog in a black triangle set in the floor of the Royal Institution in London's Faraday Museum is there because the study of frogs led directly to the electronic age.

The story starts in 1780, during a dissection being done by Italian anatomist and physician, Luigi Galvani (1737–98), who wrote:

> I had dissected and prepared a frog in the usual way... I laid it on a table on which stood an electrical machine at some distance from its conductor and separated from it by a considerable space. Now when [my assistant] ... touched accidentally and lightly the ... frog with the point of a scalpel, all the muscles of the legs seemed to contract again and again as if they were affected by powerful cramps.

Galvani had discovered that nerves transmit electrical impulses and that electricity was vital to life.

The next leap forward was taken in 1779 by Alessandro Volta (1745–1827), who repeated Galvani's experiments and then decided to make an inanimate object function in place of the frog. He replaced the frog with piles of cardboard soaked in saltwater and wired them up. Volta found this not only produced a spark, but also continued to do so without being charged. He had produced the first electric battery. Without batteries, much of our technology would not work.

The Mouth of the Beholder

When my daughter was growing up, we kept several large frogs in captivity. They ate whole adult mice. The frog would snap and grab the mouse, which would disappear in a single or double gulp. Then, while digesting the rest of the meal, the frog would sit around with the mouse tail hanging from the corner of its froggy smile. Eventually the tails would vanish, too.

I never let my daughter take any pictures of our frogs eating, even though she thought it would be cool. I told her there are zillions of photos of frogs eating things, and some are more disgusting than others. She then pointed out that if you asked our frogs what they thought about how humans eat, the frogs might have the same idea about us. Thereafter at dinner time, I imagined our frogs thinking, "Oh, look. How revolting. They cut their food up and burn it first."
– E.B.

Pregnancy tests

Starting in the 1940s, African clawed frogs, *Xenopus laevis,* were shipped around the world because they were used in human pregnancy tests. The patient's urine was injected into the frog. If the woman was indeed pregnant, the frog would begin to lay eggs. Following the development of chemical analysis for pregnancy confirmation, some frogs may have been released into the wild, where they became naturalized. Other communities of these frogs were started by pet dealers. Still others have been eradicated by state and federal agencies in the United States to keep communities from becoming established.

Research

In 1628, English physician William Harvey (1578–1657) wrote *The Anatomical Dissertation Concerning the Motion of the Heart and Blood in Animals,* based on his dissections of living frogs. Using his newly refined microscope, Anton van Leeuwenhoek (1632–1723) dissected tadpoles and described the motion of the blood through the capillaries. Jan Swammerdam (1637–80) published detailed drawings of frog muscles, testes and ovaries. Frogs were used as research subjects because they were readily available in the pre-industrial age and because they bear a great similarity to humans, in both external appearance and internal structure. Today, African clawed frogs, *Xenopus spp.,* are the "most used laboratory vertebrate" on Earth.

Skin transplants

Southeast Asian people traditionally used frog skin on wounds. Unfortunately they did not remove intestinal flat worms and other parasites before applying the skin, so the treatment sometimes worked and sometimes did more damage.

During the Soviet era, Russian doctors used frog skin to treat wounds. Vietnamese doctors observed the technique during training and first grafted frog skin onto a burn victim in 1965. By the middle 1990s, the treatment gained worldwide notice. In 2001, a plastic surgeon in Brazil presented the results of his transplants of American bullfrog skin on burn patients. He found that the frog skin speeded healing. Without frog skin, it took 20 to 30 days for scar tissue to form and cover the wound. Bullfrog skin is rich in anti-inflammatories and natural antibiotics. Using it to cover a burn reduced healing time to six days.

Vertebrate clones

Frogs have made extraordinary contributions to science, but perhaps no area owes more to frogs than cloning. In 1938, the idea of making a genetic copy of a living individual was first proposed by Hans Spemann of Germany. He was able to make an identical twin of a salamander egg. In 1952, Robert Briggs and Thomas J. King used the nuclear transfer of an embryo cell to an egg to clone northern leopard frogs, *Rana pipiens,* in Philadelphia. The next year, the structure of DNA was published by James Watson and Francis Crick.

Only a decade after the first embryo frog clones, in 1962, at Oxford University, John Gurdon cloned fertile adult African clawed frogs, *Xenopus laevis,* from cells taken from the lining of an adult frog's intestine. His frogs were the first genetically identical adult clones, but his success rate of 2 percent was so low that it is now believed that his clones came from stem cells, which naturally make up between 2 and 5 percent of all frog intestinal cells.

When Claude Met Claudia

Almost everyone who has clawed frogs, it seems, names them Claude and Claudia, then expects to be complimented on their novelty. I watched one Claude and Claudia mating. She was bigger than he; both were slippery and evaded capture. Their owner told me they breed when the water temperature drops sharply. We watched Claude and Claudia swim up to the surface together, venters up. She put out eggs that floated on the surface. He fertilized them. Claude and Claudia swam together, flowed down, swirled upward, released and fertilized eggs. They repeated this aquatic dance over and over until all the eggs were laid. Tired, they retreated to their usual solitary torpor. Their tadpoles were midwater feeders. Each had a pair of "whiskers" sprouting from the front of its face. They grew up to look just like their flat and wide, beady-eyed, web-footed parents. Who knows how many of their new owners called them Claude and Claudia, too? – E.B.

→ Dr. John Lowerison tosses an American bullfrog during a period of weightlessness. The frog assumes the parachuting posture seen in other frogs in space.

Frogs in Space

Eggs in space

The U.S. Space Program first studied animal eggs in the cramped cabins of the earliest craft, where there was little enough room for grown men. On March 16, 1966, *Gemini 8,* piloted by Neil Armstrong and David Scott, took the first frog eggs into outer space. The eggs were from northern leopard frogs, *Rana pipiens.* After the astronauts performed the first docking of two craft in space, the combined vehicle became unstable and the mission had to be terminated early. Several experiments involving the frog eggs were incomplete. When *Gemini 12* blasted off on November 11, 1966, with Jim Lovell and Edwin "Buzz" Aldrin at the controls, the refurbished frog egg division and development experiment package had plenty of time to divide and develop normally.

Frogs in space

The first frogs in space were two bullfrogs, *Rana catesbeiana,* which were blasted into outer space as part of the "Frog Ototlith Satellite (OFO-A)" on November 9, 1970. The project was planned with no hope of live recovery for the frogs. Scientists studied biometric data on the frogs and discovered that the frogs had almost adapted to weightlessness when they died.

Fertilization

Dr. Mae C. Jemison performed the first human fertilization of frog eggs in space on U.S. Space Shuttle flight STS-47 in September 1992. Four female African clawed frogs, *Xenopus laevis,* their eggs and tadpoles were kept alive in a Frog Environmental Unit. In the microgravity of the shuttle, the eggs soon developed to tadpoles. When the tadpoles returned to Earth, they swam strangely for a while until they adapted to Earth's gravity.

Zero-gravity fertilization

Automated equipment performed the first zero-gravity fertilization of vertebrate eggs in an experiment on African clawed frog, *Xenopus laevis,* eggs in a rocket experiment on May 2, 1988.

Parachuting

The first frogs on the Russian Space Station Mir accompanied the first Japanese cosmonaut in 1990. Six Japanese treefrogs, *Hyla japonica,* were observed floating in midair with all limbs extended. Cosmonauts called this behavior "parachuting." When the frogs settled on surfaces, they sat with their heads bent backward, leading researchers to wonder if they were space-sick. The frogs were studied on their return to Earth. Some of their systems were fine; others showed effects of weightlessness.

Researchers took a living frog aboard NASA's KC-135 research plane. The photo on the previous page is of Dr. John Lowerison tossing an American bullfrog, *Rana catesbeiana,* during a brief period of weightlessness on April 12, 1995. In common with the frogs on Mir, this bullfrog shows the "parachuting" posture taken by weightless frogs in space and falling frogs on Earth.

Levitation

Researchers levitated both frogs and frog embryos in 1997, using strong magnetic fields. The frogs assumed a parachuting posture similar to those photographed in orbit and in weightlessness.

Finger Food

Ceratophrys are mostly mouth and stomach. One of them decided, after not eating for several weeks, that my thumb looked like a nice food item and grabbed me while I was changing its water. They have lots of teeth! And their stomach fluids start dissolving the prey item immediately, as we discovered after prying him off my thumb and seeing the nail and skin just about gone. The doctor wanted to know, "What kind of a dog bite was this?" and I had to explain to the great merriment of the emergency room staff that this was a "frog bite," not a "dog bite." The 18 stitches dissolved the next day and black nylon was put in instead. The frog was subsequently trained to eat full-grown mice instead of human fingers, but I never put my hand in his tank again without leather work gloves! – E.B.

Glossary

aestivate, aestivation
See *estivate, estivation.*

amnion
The innermost membrane which encloses an egg. Amphibians do not have amnions and are considered anamniotic.

amphibian
Term that arose from the lifestyle of some of its members, who live on land and breed in water; hence, "to live on both sides." It is a collective term for members of the class Amphibia: salamanders, caecilians, frogs and toads.

amphibious
Term pertaining to animals of the class Amphibia, or pertaining to things that can function in water and on land.

amplexus
The clutch during breeding, in which male frogs clasp females from behind while sperm and eggs unite.

Anura, anuran
Frogs and toads are members of the order Anura; hence, anurans.

arboreal
Living or being in trees.

aquatic
Living or being in water.

batrachotoxin
A toxin produced by certain species of South American anurans.

binomial nomenclature
Each plant and animal has a unique Latinized name. The genus name, which is first, is always capitalized; the species name is in small letters. Both usually appear in italics or are underlined.

bufotoxins
The collective term for frog and toad venoms; usually produced in the parotoid gland and specifically including batrachotoxin, bufogenin, bufotenine (a hallucinogen), bufagin (with effects like digitalis on the heart), bufotalin, histrionicotoxins, pumiliotoxin and serotonin (a vasoconstrictor).

carnivorous
Meat-eating. Most adult frogs are meat-eaters (carnivores), even though most tadpoles are herbivores or scavengers. Meat-eating requires a shorter intestine than herbivory.

caudal
Referring to the tail or tail region.

chromatophore/chromatophores
Shape-changing cells in frog skin cell which contain pigments including melanophores (black), erythrophores (red), xanthophores (yellow) and iridophores (blue).

chytrid fungus
Batrochochytrium dendrobatidis; an infectious fungus that kills frogs. The earliest known frog with chytrid was a *Xenopus*, which died in 1938. It was found in a South African museum collection. Current research indicates that clawed frogs provide an asyptomatic host for the fungus, which has now been isolated from dead frogs around the world.

CITES
The Convention on International Trade in Endangered Species; an international agreement intended to regulate international trade in protected species of plants and animals. Adopted in 1975, CITES is a voluntary program in which countries may participate or not.

claspers (nuptial pads and spines)
Specialized keratin structures which develop on male amphibians that breed in water to assist them in holding slippery females during amplexus. The presence of nuptial pads is considered proof of the specimen's being an adult male in breeding condition.

class
A taxonomic group composed of one or more orders.

cranial
A collective term for the head and skull.

cranial crest
Raised, sometimes keratinized, structures along many species of toads' skulls.

crepuscular
With major activity period occurring during dusk and/or dawn.

dehydration
Loss of body fluids; also referred to as desiccation. Amphibians require appropriate humidity and moisture or they lose body fluids, dry out and desiccate.

diploid
Having two complete sets of chromosomes in the cell nucleus. Adult cells of most species are diploid.

direct development
Eggs which metamorphose to tadpoles, but do not hatch until the tadpoles transform to froglets.

diurnal
With major activity period occurring during daylight.

dorsal/dorsum
The back or top side of the frog; the side with the spinal cord. (Opposite: *venter/ventral.*)

dorsolateral folds
Ridges of skin separating the back from the side that facilitate leaping by providing extra skin for more leg motion. The presence or absence of a dorsolateral fold can tell one species from another. For example, American green frogs versus American bullfrogs, which do not have them.

ecdysis
The process of removing the outer layer of skin. Frogs and toads often eat their shed skin, which comes off in one piece from the back to the front. Also called molting and exuviation.

ectothermy/ectothermic
The process by which frogs and toads use the environment to assist in body temperature regulation. Their behaviors include basking, burrowing, hibernating and estivating. Also called poikilothermic, poikilothermous, and heterothermic.

ecosystem
The structure that results from the interaction of a physical environment and a community of organisms.

endemic
Limited in range to a specific area.

endemic species
A species that occurs only in a particular area. The opposite: cosmopolitan species are found over a wide region or area.

epidermis
The outermost layer of skin.

erythrophores
Red pigment cells contained in chromatophores.

estivate, estivation (aestivate, aestivation)
To be dormant in the hot season; the action of being dormant in the hot season.

extinct/extinction
A species that has died out leaving no heirs is considered extinct.

exuviation
See *ecdysis*.

Family
A taxonomic group that contains one or more genera.

fossorial
Adapted for burrowing and living underground.

frog spawn
Fertilized frog eggs up to the beginning of the tadpole stage.

genus/genera
A taxonomic group containing one or more species.

glycogen
An animal starch that stores fuel, usually in the liver. It is converted to glucose and then to energy as needed.

habitat
The usual place in which a frog or toad is found.

haploid
Having only one complete set of chromosomes in the cell nucleus. Sex cells, like eggs and sperm, are haploid.

herpetology, herpetologist
The study of, or one who studies, amphibians and reptiles.

hibernate, hibernation
To be dormant in the cold season; the action of being dormant in the cold season. (See *estivate, estivation*. Note: not opposite.)

introduced species
A frog or toad that has been set free in a habitat not its own, but that has naturalized by establishing residence and a breeding population. Examples include American bullfrogs in Europe, and coqui in Hawaii.

iridophores
Blue pigment cells contained in chromatophores.

keratin
A tough, waterproof protein that tips clawed frogs' fingers and toes; and forms the cranial crests and metatarsal spades of toads, as well as many other structures in frogs and toads.

keratinized
Composed of keratin.

larva/larvae
Frog and toad larvae are called tadpoles and are a free-living form that hatched from the egg and will metamorphose into an adult.

lateral
Pertaining to the side, or flank, of the body.

lateral-line organ
A sense organ peculiar to fish and amphibians which permits the animal to sense pressure changes or waves in water.

littoral
Pertaining to the shoreline or coastal area of any standing body of water.

live-bearing
In frogs and toads, when live young are produced from an egg that hatched within the body of an adult frog.

magainins
Compounds secreted by the African clawed frog; deadly to bacteria, they are being tested for their possible beneficial effects in humans.

marsupial
A term that, in the proper sense, applies only to mammals who nurse their young on teats within a pocket of skin. However, the term has been applied elsewhere in the animal kingdom; most particularly to frogs, which nurture eggs or tadpoles inside special pockets in their skins.

melanophores
Black pigment cells contained in chromatophores.

montane
Living or being in mountains or a mountainous region.

neotropical
The tropics in the New World.

nictitating membrane
A third protective fold of skin, sometimes called a third eyelid. It is transparent and can be seen down over the eyes when a frog is sleeping with its eyes open but its third eyelid shut.

nocturnal
With major activity period occurring at night.

nuptial pad
See *claspers*.

order
A taxonomic group containing one or more families.

organ
A functional and structural unit, completely different from the surrounding tissue, which is specialized for and performs a particular function.

oviparous
Egg-laying. (See *ovoviviparous* and *viviparous*, with which it should not be confused.)

ovoviviparous
Refers to eggs hatching within the body and live young emerging. (See *oviparous* and *viviparous*, with which it should not be confused.)

palette
A characteristic range of color drawn from the available pigments. In art, it may represent a certain time or school; in nature, the limits are imposed by the chemistry of the pigments themselves.

Pangaea
Periodically all the land masses on Earth unite. Pangaea was the second united continent and occupied much of the Southern Hemisphere, from about 300 to about 250 million years ago. It formed by the collision of Laurasia (in the north) with Gondwana (in the south). During the Triassic, rifting from south to north opened what we now call the Atlantic Ocean. First the rifts split South America and Africa; then, as they continued northward, North America and Europe. Earth's land masses are headed toward the third united continent, this time in the Northern Hemisphere. (See illustration on page 21.)

parotoid gland
Toxin- and/or venom-producing glands.

polyploid
Having three or more copies of each chromozone in the genome.

predator
An animal that kills and eats other animals. Most frogs and toads are predators.

pupil
The usually darkened center of an eye, which admits light.

semi-aquatic
Living or being in water part time.

species
A taxonomic group whose members can produce fertile offspring.

statoacoustic organ
A specialized organ that senses substrate vibration, aids in balance and maintains spatial control.

stochastic events
Random events such as catastrophes or especially fertile years.

tadpole
Anuran larvae; also called polliwog/pollywog (especially in the United Kingdom, Australia and New Zealand).

talus slopes
Masses of loose rocks at the base of hills or cliffs. Also called scree.

taxonomy
Classification of living things based on similarities and differences, whether structural, morphological or genetic.

tetrapod
Any four-legged vertebrate animal.

trematode
A parasitic flatworm, sometimes called a fluke, which has suckers with which it attaches to a host animal. Trematodes have complicated life-cycles; some stages occur in one or another host, or free in the environment.

tubercule, digging
Keratinized spades on the feet of some frogs and toads which are used for digging.

tympanum (singular)/tympana (plural)
A membrane in frogs and toads which covers the opening of the ear and vibrates with sound waves. Like the kettledrum with which it shares its name, it can be moved to create noise as well.

unken reflex
Some toxic animals arch their backs and tilt up their tails and chins, exposing their brightly colored undersides. The reflex is considered to be a warning to predators, since bright colors in nature often accompany a nasty chemistry set of defense toxins.

venter/ventral
The lower surface, commonly called the belly. (Opposite: *dorsal/dorsum*)

vertebrate
Having vertebrae, segmented bones forming a spinal column around a spinal cord.

vertebrates/vertebrate animals
Animals with an internal bony or cartilage skeleton, a segmented spine and a brain enclosed in a skull or cranium.

vivarium/vivaria
Artificial enclosures for the maintenance of reptiles and amphibians.

viviparous
Bearing live young from the body which have never been in a shelled egg. No frogs or toads are viviparous. (See *oviparous* and *ovoviviparous*, with which it should not be confused.)

vocal sac
One or two expandable balloons of thin skin beneath the throat in male frogs and toads which amplify breeding calls. During breeding season, the throat sacs may become bruised from constant use.

xanthophores
Yellow pigment cells contained in chromatophores.

References

Scientific and General

Amphibia Web. 2003.
elib.cs.berkeley.edu/aw/index.html

Badger, David. *Frogs*. WorldLife Library. Stillwater, MN: Voyageur Press, 2000.

Bartlett, R.D., and P.P. Bartlett. *Frogs, Toads and Treefrogs: A Complete Pet Owner's Manual*. Hauppage, NY: Barron's Educational Series, 1996.

Beddard, Frank E. *Animal Coloration: An Account of the Principal Facts and Theories Relating to the Colours and Markings of Animals*. London: Swan Sonnenschein, 1892.

Canatella, David. *Amphibian Accounts in the Tree of Life Project*, 2003. tolweb.org/tree

Cogger, Harold G., and Richard G. Zweifel. *Encyclopedia of Reptiles and Amphibians*. San Francisco: Fog City Press, 2003.

Colbert, Edwin H. *Evolution of the Vertebrates: A History of the Backboned Animals Through Time*. New York: John Wiley & Sons, Inc., 1961 (reprint).

Cooper, Sarah. *Animal Life in the Sea and on the Land: A Zoology for Young People*. New York: American Book Company, 1887.

Cope, Edward Drinker. "The Batrachia of North America." *United States National Museum Bulletin* (Number 34), 1889. Reprinted, Ashton, MD: Eric Lundberg, 1963.

Dickerson, Mary C. *The Frog Book*. New York: Doubleday, Page, 1906. (Dover Publications reprint, Mineola, NY, 1969.)

Duellman, William Edward, and Linda Trueb. *Biology of Amphibians*. New York: McGraw-Hill, 1986.

——. *Biology of Amphibians*. Baltimore: Johns Hopkins University Press, 1994.

Feder, Martin E., and Warren W. Burggren, eds. *Environmental Physiology of the Amphibians*. Chicago: University of Chicago Press, 1992.

Frost, Darrel (Curator of Reptiles, American Museum of Natural History). *Amphibian Species of the World: An Online Reference*, 2005. research.amnh.org/herpetology/amphibia

Halliday, Tim, and Kraig Adler. *The Firefly Encyclopedia of Reptiles and Amphibians*. Toronto: Firefly Books, 2002.

——. *All the World's Animals: Reptiles and Amphibians*. New York: Torstar Books, 1986.

——. *The Encyclopedia of Reptiles and Amphibians.* New York: Facts on File, 1986.

Hofrichter, Robert, ed. *Amphibians: The World of Frogs, Toads, Salamanders and Newts.* Toronto: Firefly Books, 2000.

Holmes, Samuel J. *The Biology of the Frog* (3rd edition). New York: Macmillan, 1920.

Mackenzie, Fred T. *Our Changing Planet: An Introduction to Earth System Science and Global Environmental Change.* Upper Saddle River, NJ: Prentice Hall, 1995.

Parsons, Harry. *The Nature of Frogs: Amphibians with Attitude.* Vancouver, BC: Douglas & McIntyre/ Greystone Books, 2000.

Peters, J. *Dictionary of Herpetology.* New York: Hafner Publishing, 1964.

Speare, Rick, and Lee Berger. *Global Distribution of Chytridiomycosis in Amphibians* (updated 2002). www.jcu.edu.au/school/phtm/PHTM/frogs/chyglob. htm

Stebbins, Robert C., and Nathan W. Cohen. *Natural History of Amphibians.* Princeton, NJ: Princeton University Press, 1995.

Swingland, Ian, Roger Avery, Roger Thorpe, Richard Tinsley, and ICE Staff. *Programme, First World Congress of Herpetology, 11-19 September 1989.* Canterbury, UK: University of Kent at Canterbury, 1989.

Tenney, Sanborn, and Abby A. Tenney. *Natural History of Animals.* New York: Scribner, Armstrong, 1872.

Tyler, Michael J. *Australian Frogs: A Natural History.* Ithaca, NY: Cornell University Press, 1994.

Vial, James L. *Evolutionary Biology of the Anurans: Contemporary Research on Major Problems.* Columbia, MO: University of Missouri Press, 1973.

Wiley, E.O., *et al. The Compleat Cladist: A Primer of Phylogenetic Procedures.* Special Publication 19. Lawrence, KS: University of Kansas, Museum of Natural History, October 1991.

Wright, Albert Hazen, and Anna Allen Wright. *Handbook of Frogs and Toads of the United States and Canada* (3rd edition). Ithaca, NY: Comstock Publishing, 1949.

Literary

Aesop. *Aesop's Fables: The Frogs Desiring a King.* Aesop Online Collection (translations by Rev. George F. Townsend, Ambrose Bierce and others). www.AesopFables.com

Aristophanes. *The Frogs* (405 BCE). Translated by Ian Johnston. www.mala.bc.ca/~johnstoi/aristophanes/ frogs.htm

Boccaccio, Giovanni. *The Decameron. Fourth Day, seventh novel* (1351 – 53). University of Adelaide, Australia Electronic Books. etext.library.adelaide.edu. au/b/boccaccio/giovanni/b664d/

Dickinson, Emily. *I'm Nobody! Who Are You? Poems of Emily Dickinson for Children.* Owings Mills, MD: Stemmer House, 1978.

Grahame, Kenneth. *The Wind in the Willows.* New York: Charles Scribner's Sons, 1980.

Homer. *The Homeric Hymns, and The Battle of The Frogs and the Mice* (*Batrachomyomachia*, 800 BCE). Translated by Daryl Hine. New York: Atheneum, 1972.

Lupton, Thomas. *A Thousand Notable Things* (1579). Quoted in *Forgotten English* (Jeffrey Kacirk, New York: Morrow, 1997).

Shakespeare, William. *The Tragedy of Macbeth.* In *The Complete Works of William Shakespeare* (Cambridge text), edited by William Aldis Wright. Garden City, NY: Doubleday, 1936.

Twain, Mark. "The Celebrated Jumping Frog of Calaveras County." In *The Celebrated Jumping Frog, and Other Sketches.* New York: C.H. Webb, 1867.

Vasishtha. *Rig Vida. Hymn 103, Frogs.* Translated by Ralph T.H. Griffith, 1896. www.sacred-texts.com/ hin/rigveda/rv07103.htm

Photo Credits

Index

fire-bellied toads, 31–32, 75, 87, 91
    European, *31*, 31–32, *32*
    Oriental, *31*, 32
First World Congress of Herpetology, 109
fish, 20, 34, 35, 70
Flectonotus, 50
    pygmaeus, 50
flying frogs, 71, *71*, 83, 149
forearm signaling, 90
forests, clear-cutting of, 64, 69, 73, 114, 121
fossils, 19–21, *20*, *21*, 22, 24–25, *25*, 30, 105, 147
    Archaeobatrachia, 29, 32
    Mesobatrachia, 33, 35, 36, 37
    Neobatrachia, 40, 47, 52, 55, 56, 65
freeze-tolerant species, 11, 85, 96, 148
frog-leg trade, 69, 107–108, 110
frogs and toads, differences between, 13, 38, 40–41
fungal disease, 118–119
fungicides, 112

G

Galvani, Luigi, 80, 150
gamelan frog, 65
gastric-brooding frogs, 57, 110, 112
Gastrophryne, 65
    carolinensis, 65
    olivacea, 65, *65*
Gastrotheca, 50, *144*
    ovifera, *49*
geological time column, 19
ghost frogs, 55, 75
    Cape, 55
    Hewitt's, 55
    Natal, 55
    Table Mountain, 55
giant toad. *See* marine toad
gills, 50, 84, 98
glass frogs, 44–45, 75
    bare-hearted, *45*
    Fleischmann's, *44*
    La Palma, *84*, *100*
gliding, 67, 71, 83
global warming, 110, 112, 122
gold frog, 39, *39*, 148
    Brazilian, 39
golden frog, Panamanian, 113, *135*
Goliath frog, 67, 68–69, *146*, 148
gopher frog, 95
Grahame, Kenneth, 139
green and golden bell frog, 87
green frog, Indian, 69, 150

greenhouse frog, 53, 125
ground frogs, Australian, 58, 75
Gurdon, John, 151
Gymnophiona, 22

H

habitat, 25, 29, 41, 105, 106
    destruction of, 64, 110, 112, 114, 121, 144
hairy frog, 59, *59*, 149
Hamilton's frog, 30
harlequin frogs, *42*, 43
    Rancho Grande, 144
Harvey, William, 151
hearing, 24, 25, 90, 91
heart, 84
Heleioporus australiacus, 87
Heleophryne, 55
    hewitti, 55
    natalensis, 55
    purcelli, 55
    rosei, 55
Heleophrynidae, 55, 74–75
Hemiphractus proboscideus, 48, *49*
Hemisotidae, 62
Hemisus, 62
    marmoratus, 62, *62*
Henson, Jim, 140
herbicides, 112
hibernation, 32, 85, 96, 97, 121
hognose snake, 94–95
Hogsback frog, 68
Homer, 131
Hoplobatrachus tigerinus, 69, *76*
hormones, 81, 100, 112
horned frog
    Argentine, 52
    Malayan, *33*, *36*, 36, *108*
human use of frogs. *See also* culture
    as food, 17, 46, 69, 79, 107–108, 110, 113, 117
    in medical research, 35, 94, 152
    as pets, 31
    in pregnancy tests, 35, 152
    in scientific experiments, 31, 79–80, 96, 108, 115,
        120, 145, 150, 151, 152, 153
humidity, response to, 88, 89
hunting, 41, 82, 85, 86, 88, 97
Hyalinobatrachium, 44
    colymbiphyllum, 45
    fleischmanni, 44
    valerioi, *84*, *100*
    vireovittatum, 45